Teacher Man

FRANK McCOURT

Level 4

Retold by Chris Rice
Series Editors: Andy Hopkins and Jocelyn Potter

D0732587

Pearson Education Limited

Edinburgh Gate, Harlow,
Essex CM20 2JE, England
and Associated Companies throughout the world.

ISBN: 978-1-4058-8233-0

Published by arrangement with
HarperCollins Publishers Ltd
© Frank McCourt 2005

First published 2007
This edition published 2008

Text copyright © Pearson Education Ltd 2008

3 5 7 9 10 8 6 4

Set in 11/14pt Bembo
Printed in China
SWTC/03

Published by Pearson Education Limited in association with
Penguin Books Ltd, both companies being subsidiaries of Pearson PLC

Acknowledgements

Every effort has been made to trace the copyright holders and we apologise in advance
for any unintentional omissions. We would be pleased to insert the appropriate
acknowledgement in any subsequent edition of this publication.

We are grateful to the following for permission to reproduce this photograph:
pgviii AFP/Getty Images

For a complete list of the titles available in the Penguin Readers series please write to your local
Pearson Longman office or to: Penguin Readers Marketing Department, Pearson Education,
Edinburgh Gate, Harlow, Essex CM20 2JE

Contents

Introduction

Petey threw his brown-paper sandwich bag at Andy, and the class cheered excitedly. The bag landed on the floor between the blackboard and Andy's desk.

I came from behind my desk and made the first sound of my teaching career: "Hey."

They ignored me. I moved toward Petey and made my first teacher statement: "Stop throwing sandwiches."

Petey and the class looked shocked.

This is how Frank McCourt's teaching career begins—and it doesn't get easier! As a young man, Frank McCourt leaves his poor, miserable childhood in Ireland behind him and moves to New York. He works hard and studies hard, and soon becomes a teacher in a school where the students have no interest in learning. Many of them are almost impossible to teach, with terrible problems at home and in school. McCourt is faced with students like Kevin Dunne, who nobody wants to teach, and Serena, who causes many problems but, in the end, almost makes him cry with happiness. There is Hector, who thinks that his teacher is just another crazy, drunk, violent Irishman, and Andrew, who angers McCourt but who knows a secret about his teacher's past.

For thirty years, from the 1950s to the 1980s, McCourt sails the stormy seas of the New York education system. His stories of classrooms, meetings with parents, disagreements with principals, his own personal problems, and his hopes for the future are all beautifully described. How will this caring, book-loving man with his poor Irish childhood and low self-confidence survive the classrooms of New York? What effect will his own special, unusual way of teaching have on the bored, angry, confused students in his classes? And what effect will *they* have on *him*? This is a true story.

Many readers may be surprised by the problems that Frank McCourt finds in the classrooms of New York. Even today, when more than 85% of adults in the U.S. have completed high school and 27% have a university degree, there are many Americans who have difficulty reading and writing. McCourt's experiences in the second half of the last century are sad, amusing, interesting, and entertaining, but they paint a thoughtful, often frightening, picture of the expectations and realities of poor Americans.

There are two main types of high school in the U.S.: public and private. About 10% of students go to private schools. The others go to schools which are paid for by the government. Students have to complete twelve years of education before they can go to college or university. When McCourt was teaching, there were many excellent public high schools—like Stuyvesant High School in New York, where he taught for a time. But there were many others—vocational high schools—which suffered from financial difficulties, poor conditions, and low levels of success.

McCourt spends his first years as a teacher in these vocational schools. He tries to interest his students in literature and ideas, but it is difficult. The students want to leave school and earn money as secretaries, hairdressers, or dock workers. In many ways, these are unhappy years for McCourt because he thinks that he is failing. But in other ways, they are a great success. His own difficult childhood helps him understand his students' problems, and his special gifts as a teacher bring surprising, often amusing, results.

Frank McCourt was born in Brooklyn, New York, in 1930, but went to Ireland when he was four years old. There, he had a tough, poor, miserable childhood. His father, Malachy, was usually unemployed, and when he was earning, he spent much of the money on alcohol. His mother, Angela, had to beg for money from churches to feed her children. Frank became very sick and almost died. While he was in the hospital, he was able to eat regular meals for the first time—and there were books to read. He first read Shakespeare in the hospital, and McCourt remembers the importance of this in his first book, *Angela's Ashes* (1996): "I don't know what it means and I don't care because it's Shakespeare and it's like having jewels in my mouth when I say the words."

When he was nineteen years old, McCourt returned to New York and earned a degree from New York University. That was the beginning of his career as an English teacher. *Angela's Ashes*, which describes his childhood in Ireland, came out when he was sixty-six years old and has been made into a movie. Although it is a sad, often upsetting story, it contains scenes of powerful beauty and humor. The book was a great success, and McCourt received the famous Pulitzer Prize for it in 1997. His second book, *'Tis* (1999) continues the story of his life, and his third book, *Teacher Man* (2005), describes his life and experiences as a New York school teacher.

His brother, Malachy, is also a writer. Together they wrote the stage play *A Couple of Blaguards*, about their childhood experiences.

Frank McCourt

Chapter 1 Teaching

If I knew anything about psychology, I'd be able to blame all my troubles on my miserable childhood in Ireland. That terrible childhood took away my confidence and filled me with self-pity; it made me afraid of my emotions, jealous of other people, unable to obey orders, and frightened of the opposite sex. It also stopped me from making progress in the world and made me unfit, almost, for human society. So, it's surprising that I ever managed to become a teacher. I'm very proud of surviving all those years in the classrooms of New York. There should be special prizes for people who have survived miserable childhoods and become teachers.

When I taught in New York City high schools for thirty years, no one listened to me except my students. Outside the school I was so unimportant that no one noticed me. Then I wrote a book about my childhood, and I was suddenly famous. When the book became a best-seller and was translated into thirty languages, I couldn't believe it.

My first book, *Angela's Ashes*, came out in 1996 when I was sixty-six. The second, *'Tis*, came out in 1999 when I was sixty-nine. My new writer-friends had written their first books when they were in their twenties. So, why did it take me so long?

I was teaching, that's why. Not in college or university, where you have plenty of time for writing and other activities, but in four different New York City public high schools. When you teach five high school classes a day, five days a week, you're too tired to go home and write great literature. After a day of five classes, your head is filled with the noise of the classroom.

In *'Tis* I wrote about my life in America and how I became a teacher. After it came out, I felt guilty that I hadn't talked enough about teaching. In America, doctors, lawyers, army officers, actors, television people, and politicians are admired and rewarded. Not teachers. Teachers are spoken to politely but they aren't respected; they're congratulated on having such long vacations. When teachers stop working, they disappear into the shadows, hoping that one child will remember them. Keep dreaming, teacher. You won't be celebrated.

◆

You imagine a future filled with success. Your lessons will be perfect; your students will be pleasantly surprised. Principals and other important people will hear the sounds of excitement from your room. You'll win prizes: Teacher of the Year, Teacher of the Century. You'll be invited to Washington. President Eisenhower will shake your hand. Newspapers will ask you, an ordinary teacher, for your opinion on education. This will be big news: a teacher is asked for his opinion. Wow! You'll be on television.

Television.

Imagine: A teacher on television.

They'll fly you to Hollywood, where you'll star in movies about your own life. But this won't be the end of the story. After evenings in the company of the most beautiful female movie stars, you'll discover the emptiness of their lives. You'll listen guiltily as they tell you how much they admire you. You've become a Hollywood star because of your caring attitude toward your students. And they, the beautiful movie stars, are ashamed of the uselessness of their Hollywood lives. If they left Hollywood, they, too, could enjoy the rewarding pleasures of teaching the future dock workers, typists, and store assistants of America. It must feel wonderful, they say, to work every day with the young people of America. Your low pay is unimportant. Your real reward is the light in your students' eyes as they bring you gifts from their grateful and admiring parents: cookies, bread, and home-made wine from the mothers and fathers of your one hundred and seventy students of McKee Vocational High School, Staten Island, in the City of New York.

Chapter 2   A Sandwich Situation

It is March 1958. I sit at my desk in an empty classroom in McKee High School. In a minute the bell will ring, and the students will rush in. What will they say if they see me at the desk? "Hey, look. He's hiding." They know everything about teachers. You sit at the desk because you're scared or lazy. You're using the desk as a wall. You should get out there and stand. Be a man. If you make one mistake on your first day, your students will remember it for months.

The kids are sixteen years old. They've been in school for eleven years. So, teachers come, teachers go. But kids watch, study, judge. They know body language, voice, general attitude, and appearance. They don't discuss these things with each other. After eleven years, they just know, and they pass the information on to the next group.

It's a mistake to arrive early. It gives you too much time to think about what's going to happen. Where did I get the idea that I was brave enough to face American teenagers? Stupidity. These are the 1950s and newspapers report the unhappiness of young Americans. They have no hope. Life is meaningless. All adults are dishonest. What's the purpose of life?

They're so unhappy that they join gangs and fight other gangs. If one of them dies, there's great public anger, and schools and teachers are blamed for not doing their jobs.

♦

Vocational schools were seen as places for students who were not smart enough for other high schools. They weren't respected. It didn't matter to the public that thousands of young people wanted to be mechanics, machine operators, or electricians. Those young people didn't want to learn about history, art, or literature.

But kids thought, "If we have to sit in these boring classes, we'll do it. We'll try to be nice to the teachers for four years, and then we'll be free."

Here they are. The door hits the wall with a loud noise. Why can't they just walk into the room, say, "Good morning," and sit? Oh, no. They have to shout and push. One says, "Hey," in a playfully violent way, and another one says, "Hey," in reply. They insult each other, ignore the late bell, and are in no hurry to sit down. Look, there's a new teacher up there and new teachers don't know anything. So? Bell? Teacher? New guy. Who is he? Who cares?

They talk to friends across the room, sit lazily in desks that are too small for them, stretch out their legs, laugh if someone falls over them. They stare out the window or over my head at the American flag. They cut their names on desk tops with small knives next to where their fathers cut *their* names long ago. Couples sit together, hold hands, whisper, and look lovingly into each other's eyes. Three boys at the back tilt their chairs against the closets and sing pop songs, telling the world that they're just teenagers in love.

Five times a day they push into the room. Five classes, thirty to thirty-five in each class. Teenagers? In Ireland we saw them in American movies—angry-looking, never smiling, driving around in cars—and we wondered why they were angry and unsmiling. They had food and clothes and money, and they were still mean to their parents. There were no teenagers in Ireland, not in my world. You were a child. You went to school until you were fourteen. If you weren't polite to your parents, they hit you across the face with a belt. You grew up, got a boring job, got married, drank your beer on a Friday night, and kept your wife busy with babies. In a few years you went to England to work as a builder or to join the army.

◆

The problem of the sandwich started when a boy named Petey asked the class, "Does anyone want a sandwich?"

"Are you joking?" laughed a boy named Andy. "Your mother must hate you, giving you cold-meat sandwiches like that."

Petey threw his brown-paper sandwich bag at Andy, and the class cheered excitedly. The bag landed on the floor between the blackboard and Andy's desk.

I came from behind my desk and made the first sound of my teaching career: "Hey."

They ignored me. I moved toward Petey and made my first teacher statement: "Stop throwing sandwiches."

Petey and the class looked shocked. This teacher, this new teacher, just stopped a good fight. New teachers should look the other way or send for the principal.

Benny called out from the back of the room. "Hey, teacher man, he already threw the sandwich."

The class laughed. One boy covered his mouth and said, "Stupid," and I knew he was talking about me. I wanted to knock him out of his seat, but that would be the end of my teaching career. Also, he was enormous.

The class waited. What would this new teacher do?

Professors of education at New York University never taught you how to manage flying-sandwich situations. Should I say, "Hey, Petey, come here and pick up that sandwich?" Should I pick it up myself and throw it into the wastepaper basket? They had to recognize I was boss. I was strong. I wasn't going to accept this kind of behavior.

I picked up the sandwich, took it out of its bag, and ate it. It was my first act of classroom management. Thirty-four boys and girls stared at me in shocked silence. I could see the admiration in their eyes. They'd never seen a teacher pick up a sandwich from the floor and eat it in front of the class before. Sandwich man.

When I'd finished, I made a ball of the paper bag and threw it into the wastepaper basket. The class cheered. "Wow," they said. "Did you see *that*? He eats the sandwich. He hits the basket. Wow."

I felt in total control of the classroom. I could do nothing wrong. Fine, except I didn't know what to do next. I was there to teach English, and wondered how to move from a sandwich situation to spelling or grammar.

My students smiled until they saw the principal's face in the door window. He opened the door and said, "A word, Mr. McCourt?"

Petey whispered, "Hey, mister. Don't worry about the sandwich."

The class said, "Yeah, yeah," to show me that they were on my side if I had trouble with the principal.

Outside the classroom, he said, "I'm sure you understand, Mr. McCourt, that teachers shouldn't eat their lunch at nine o'clock in the morning in their classrooms in front of these boys and girls. It gives children the wrong idea. What would happen if all the teachers began to eat their lunches in class, especially in the morning? We have enough trouble trying to stop the *kids* eating in class."

I wanted to tell him the truth about the sandwich and how well I'd managed the situation. I wanted to say that it wasn't my sandwich. But if I did, it might be the end of my teaching career. So I said nothing.

The principal said he was there to help me because, ha, ha, I seemed to need help. "I agree you had their full attention," he said. "But can you do it in a different way? Try teaching. That's why you're here, young man. Teaching. Now that's all. Remember, no eating in class for teacher or students."

I said, "Yes, sir," and he waved me back to the classroom.

The class said, "What did he say?"

"He said I shouldn't eat my lunch in the classroom at nine o'clock in the morning."

"That's unfair. You weren't eating lunch."

Petey said, "I'll tell my mom you liked her sandwich."

"All right, Petey, but don't tell her you threw it away."

"No, no. She'd kill me. She's from Sicily. They get excited over there in Sicily."

"Tell her it was the most delicious sandwich I ever had in my life."

"OK."

Chapter 3   A Problem with Sheep

It was my fault. Instead of teaching, I told stories because stories kept the kids quiet and in their seats. In the teachers' cafeteria the more experienced teachers warned me, "Son, tell them nothing about yourself. They're kids, remember. You're the teacher. Don't tell them about your private life. They're not your natural friends. They can smell it when you're going to teach a real lesson on grammar. They'll know if you're even thinking about grammar or spelling. They'll put up their hands and ask you about your childhood and your hobbies. If you're not careful, you'll answer all their questions. They'll go home without knowing anything about grammar but knowing everything about your life. They'll carry bits and pieces of your private life in their heads forever, and you'll never get them back. Your life, man. It's all you have. Tell them nothing."

The advice was wasted. I had to learn about these things in my own way.

◆

On my second day at McKee a boy asks a question that sends me into the past. It affects the way that I teach for the next thirty years.

Joey Santos calls out, "Hey, teacher man …"

"Call me Mr. McCourt."

"Yeah. OK. So, are you Scottish or something?"

"No. I'm not Scottish. I'm Irish."

Joey looks interested. "Oh, yeah? What's Irish?"

I talk about Ireland for a short time, but there are other questions. Don't let them control the classroom. Be strong. Show them who's boss. Tell them, "Open your notebooks. Time for the spelling list."

"Oh, teacher, oh man. Spelling? Do we have to? B-o-r-i-n-g spelling list." They pretend to hit their heads on desks, hide their faces in their arms. They beg to go to the bathroom. "We thought you were a nice guy. Why do all these English teachers have to do the same old thing? Same old spelling lessons, same old vocabulary lessons, same old garbage. Can't you tell us more about Ireland?"

"Hey, teacher man." Joey again.

"Joey, I told you my name is Mr. McCourt."

"Yeah, yeah. So, mister, did you go out with girls in Ireland?"

"No! We went out with sheep. What do you think we went out with?"

There's an explosion of laughing. "This teacher. Crazy. Talks funny. Goes out with sheep. Lock up your sheep."

"Excuse me. Open your notebooks, please. We have a spelling list to do."

More laughing. "Will sheep be on the list?"

I thought my answer had been smart, but it was a mistake. There'll be trouble. Some students will certainly report me. "Oh, Mom, oh, Dad, oh, Mr. Principal, guess what teacher said in class today. Bad things about sheep."

I'm not ready for this. It's not teaching. When will I be tough enough to walk into the room, get their immediate attention, and teach? Around this school there are quiet, serious classes where teachers are in control. In the cafeteria older teachers tell me, "Yeah, it takes at least five years."

Next day the principal sends for me. He sits behind his desk, smoking a cigarette, repeating into the telephone, "I'm sorry. It won't happen again. New teacher, I'm afraid. I'll speak to him."

He puts the phone down. "Sheep. What's this about sheep?"

"Sheep?"

"I don't know what to do with you. There are complaints about you. First the sandwich, now the sheep. My phone doesn't stop ringing. Parents are really angry. You've been in the building for two days, and for two days you've been in trouble. How do you do it? Why did you have to tell these kids about the sheep?"

"I'm sorry. They kept asking me questions, and I was angry. They were only trying to keep me away from the spelling list. I thought the sheep thing was funny at the time."

"Thirteen parents want me to fire you."

"I was only joking."

"No, young man. No jokes here. You're the teacher. When you say something to the kids, they believe every word."

"I'm sorry."

"This time I'll forget it. I'll tell the parents you've just got off the boat from Ireland and don't understand American ways."

"But I was born here."

"Could you be quiet for one minute and listen while I save your life? This time you won't be punished. If you want to go up in this system—principal, assistant principal, guidance counselor— you have to be more careful."

"Sir, I don't want to be principal. I just want to teach."

"Yeah, yeah, they all say that. You'll soon understand. These kids will give you gray hair before you're thirty."

♦

It was clear that I had different ideas about teaching. I didn't like classes where the lesson was king and the students were nothing. That reminded me of my school in Ireland.

Why couldn't the principal invite me to do what I wanted with the class? Then I could tell the students to lie on the floor and go to sleep.

"What?"

"I said, 'Go to sleep.'"

"Why?"

"Think about it while you're lying on the floor."

They'd lie on the floor. I'd ask a girl to sing a gentle song. Everything would get quiet. The bell would ring, and they'd be slow off the floor. They'd leave the room, relaxed and puzzled. Please don't ask me why I'd do that with them. I just would.

Chapter 4   Stories

"So, teacher, how did you come to America?"

I tell them about my return to America when I was nineteen. I had no idea I'd ever become a teacher. I never dreamed I could climb so high in the world. Except for one new book in my suitcase, everything about me was old and had been used before. Everything in my head was old, too. Parents, teachers, and churchmen had filled it with religion and Ireland's long sad history of pain and suffering. I told them about my first years in New York, working in low-paid jobs. Then my two years in the army. After that I went to college to become a teacher.

"So, Mr. McCourt, what was it like growing up in Ireland?"

I'm twenty-seven years old, satisfying these American teenagers with journeys into my past. I never thought my past would be useful. Why would anybody want to know about my miserable life? Then I realize my father did the same thing when he told us stories by the fire. I have arguments with myself. I'm telling stories but I should be teaching.

I *am* teaching. Storytelling is teaching.

Storytelling is a waste of time.

What can I do? I can't teach any other way.

You're dishonest. You're cheating our children.

They don't seem to think so.

I'm a teacher in an American school telling stories of my childhood in Ireland. They learn about my three brothers. My father, who was always drunk, left us when I was ten years old. A baby sister died; twin boys died. My mother begged for food and clothes, but she refused to let anyone take us away from her. A rich lady once offered to buy her baby, my brother Malachy, but she said no. Years later, I told her she was wrong not to sell Malachy. Without Malachy, I said, there'd be more food for the rest of us. My mother replied, "Well, I offered her you, but she wasn't interested."

Girls in the class say, "Oh, Mr. McCourt, that was wrong of your mother. People shouldn't offer to sell their children. You're not so ugly."

Boys in the class say, "Well, he's not very handsome, either. Only joking, Mr. McCourt. You got any more stories?"

"No, no more stories. This is an English class. Parents are complaining."

"Oh, Mr. McCourt, tell us how you became a teacher."

I tell them about my four years at New York University. I worked nights to help pay for my course. I was always tired. I fell asleep in libraries. The Professor of Education warned us about the difficult days ahead. I learned that teaching could be complicated. I learned about lesson plans and different methods of teaching. I had a bitter experience with love. I liked my girlfriend,

11

June, very much, but I left her because she had lots of other boyfriends. I could never understand why she behaved like that. In the end, I managed to get my teacher's license.

"Hey, Mr. McCourt, did you ever do real work? Not teaching, but, you know, real work?"

"Are you joking? Teaching is harder than working on the docks. How many of you have relatives working along the waterfront?"

Half the class—mostly Italian, a few Irish.

Before I came to this school I worked on the Manhattan, Hoboken, and Brooklyn docks because it was difficult for me to find a teaching job. Schools told me, "Sorry, your accent's going to be a problem. What will parents say when their kids come home from school with Irish accents?" Work on the docks was easier. While you were working with your body, your brain had a vacation. But it was often rough. There were fights and I learned to be brave.

When I tell stories about the docks, the kids look at me in a different way. One boy says it's strange to have a teacher who worked like a normal person. The boy says he used to think he wanted to work on the docks because the money was good. You could steal things easily. But his father was angry with him, and you don't argue with your father in an Italian family. His father said, "If this Irishman can become a teacher, you can, too. Forget the docks. You might make money but what good is that when you can't straighten your back?"

Chapter 5   Open Day

Twice a year at McKee we had Open School Day and Open School Night, when parents visited the school to see how their children were progressing. Teachers sat in classrooms talking to parents or listening to their complaints. Most visiting parents were mothers because that was the job of the woman, but sometimes a whole family might come to visit the teacher, and the room was crowded with fathers, mothers, and small children. The women talked to each other in a friendly way, but the men sat quietly at the desks.

My first time at McKee, I had a student monitor, Norma, who organized the parents waiting to see me.

First, I had to get past the subject of my accent, especially with the women. When I opened my mouth, they said, "Oh, my God, what a nice accent." Then they told me about their grandparents, who'd also come from Ireland. They wanted to know everything about me. They said it was wonderful I was a teacher because most Irish people became policemen or worked in churches. Finally, they asked how their little Harry was doing.

I had to be careful if the dad was sitting there. If I criticized Harry, the dad might go home and hit him. If other students heard about it, they'd learn not to trust me. I was learning that teachers and kids have to help each other in front of parents, principals, and the world in general.

I said positive things about all my students. They paid attention, they were never late, they were enthusiastic, they all had a bright future, and the parents should be pleased. Dad and Mom looked at each other with a proud smile. Or they were puzzled and said, "Are you sure you're talking about our kid? Our Harry?"

"Oh, yes. Harry."

"Does he behave himself in class? Is he polite?"

"Oh, yes. He always has something to say in our discussions."

"Oh, yeah? That's not the Harry we know. He must be different in school because at home he's an unpleasant little animal. He doesn't say a word at home. Never does anything. He just listens to pop music all day." The dad hated pop music. Elvis Presley was the worst thing that America ever produced. He wanted to throw the record player in the trash.

Other parents became impatient and asked if we could stop talking about Elvis Presley. Harry's parents told them to stop complaining and wait. It was a free country, and nobody was going to interrupt their interview with this nice teacher from Ireland.

But the other parents said, "Hurry up. We haven't got all night. We're working people, too."

I didn't know what to do. I said thank you to the parents, hoping they would leave. But the dad said angrily, "Hey, we're not finished yet."

Norma, my student monitor, understood my problem and took control of the situation. She calmly passed around a sheet of paper for the parents' names and phone numbers. "Mr. McCourt will contact you," she said.

The parents stopped complaining and congratulated Norma on her intelligence. "You should be a teacher yourself," they said. She told them she had no interest in being a teacher. She wanted to work for a travel company and get free tickets everywhere. One mother said, "Oh, you don't want to stay at home with a family and kids? You'd be a great mother."

Then Norma said the wrong thing. "No," she said, "I don't want kids. Kids are terrible. You have to wash them and feed them and then come to school to see how they're doing and you're never free."

A few minutes ago parents were congratulating her on her intelligence. Now they felt insulted by her opinions on parents and kids. One father angrily destroyed the sheet of paper with the names and phone numbers. He threw it toward the front of the room where I sat. He picked up his coat and told his wife, "Let's get out of here. This place is a madhouse." His wife shouted at me, "Don't you have any control over these kids? If this one was my daughter, I'd beat her. She shouldn't insult the mothers of America like that."

My face burned with embarrassment. I wanted to apologize to the parents in the room and the mothers of America. I wanted to tell Norma, "Go away. You've ruined my first Open School Day." She stood by the door calmly saying goodnight to the parents, pretending not to notice their angry stares. Now what should I do? Where was the book by a professor of education that could help? Fifteen parents still sat in the room waiting to hear about their sons and daughters. What should I say to them?

Norma spoke again and my heart began to sink. "Ladies and gentlemen, I did a stupid thing and I'm so sorry. It wasn't Mr. McCourt's fault. He's a good teacher. He's new, you know, just here a few months, so he's just a learning teacher. I was wrong to say those things because I got him into trouble and I'm sorry."

Then she began to cry and a number of mothers rushed toward her while I sat at my desk. It was Norma's job to call the parents up, one by one, but she was surrounded by a group of mothers. I didn't know what to do. Should I act independently and say, "Next?" The parents seemed more interested in Norma than in the future of their children. When the end-of-meeting bell rang, they smiled and left, saying this visit with me had been nice, and good luck in my teaching career.

♦

Maybe Paulie's mother was right. On my second Open School Day she told me I was a cheat. She was proud of her Paulie, future electrician, nice kid who planned to start his own business one day. He wanted to marry a nice girl, have a family, and stay out of trouble.

I was angry with her. But, at the back of my head a little voice filled me with doubt. Maybe I was a cheat. Maybe I wasn't a good teacher.

"I ask my kid about his day in school, and he tells me about stories of Ireland and you coming to New York. Stories, stories,

stories. You know what you are? A cheat. And I'm saying that kindly, trying to help."

I wanted to be a good teacher. I wanted to fill my students' heads with spelling and vocabulary. I wanted to help them have a better life, but I didn't know how.

The mother said she was Irish, married to an Italian, and could see all my secrets. She knew my game. When I told her I agreed with her she said, "Ooh, you agree with me? You actually know you're a cheat?"

"I'm just trying to do my best. They ask me questions about my life and I answer them. They don't listen when I try to teach English. They look out the window. They sleep. They eat sandwiches. They want the bathroom."

"Why don't you teach them what they need to learn—spelling and big words? What will my son, Paulie, do when he goes out into the big world and he can't use big words?"

I told Paulie's mother that I hoped to be a good teacher one day, confident in the classroom. But until then, I was going to continue trying. I don't know why, but that made her emotional. She started crying and looked in her handbag for a handkerchief. I offered her mine, but she shook her head and asked, "Who does your washing? That's the saddest-looking gray handkerchief I've ever seen in my life. Your shoes, too. I've never seen such sad shoes. No woman would ever let you buy shoes like them. It's easy to see you've never been married."

She brushed the tears from her eyes with the back of her hand. "Do you think my Paulie can spell handkerchief?"

"I don't think so. It's not on the list."

"Do you see what I mean? You people have no idea. You don't have handkerchief on the list, but he'll need handkerchiefs all his life. Every day Paulie comes home telling us these stories and we don't need to hear them. We've got our own troubles. It's easy to see that you're new in this country …"

"No, I'm not new in this country. I was born here. I was in the army here. I worked on the docks. I graduated from New York University."

"See?" she said. "That's what I mean. I ask you a simple question and you give me the story of your life. Be careful, Mr. McCurd. These kids don't need to know the life story of every teacher in the school. Just give them spelling and words, Mr. McCurd, and the parents of this school will thank you forever. Forget the storytelling. If we want stories, we've got a *TV Guide* at home."

Chapter 6   Grammar and Gibberish

I thought about what Paulie's mother said and realized it was time to take control. Organization is everything. I wanted to start again, make plans for every lesson. I was the captain of this ship, and I was going to choose its direction.

"No more stories," I told my students. "Your English teacher is going to teach English and won't be stopped by little teenage tricks. Take out your notebooks. That's right, your notebooks."

I wrote on the board, "John went to the store."

There was a storm of complaints. "What's he doing to us? English teachers are all the same. Old John goes to the store again."

"All right. What's the subject of this sentence? Yes, Mario?"

"That's easy. It's all about a guy who wants to go to the store."

"Yes, yes, that's what the sentence is about. But what's the subject? It's one word. Yes, Donna."

"I think Mario is right. It's all about …"

"No, Donna. The subject here is one word."

"What do you mean?"

"What's the problem? Aren't you studying Spanish? Don't you have grammar in Spanish? Doesn't Miss Grober tell you the parts of a sentence?"

"Yeah, but she's not always bothering us about John going to the store."

My head felt hot and I wanted to shout, "Why are you so stupid? Why do I have to waste my time with you when outside spring birds are singing in the morning sun? Why do I have to look at your silly, bad-tempered faces? You're not hungry. You're well-clothed and warm. You're getting a free high school education and you're not even slightly grateful. Learn the parts of a sentence. Am I asking too much? Why can't you just look at this sentence and, for the first time in your miserable teenage existence, try to learn?"

But they were smart. They had a mysterious way of knowing that "John went to the store" was the limit of my grammatical knowledge. I gave them a serious look and sat at my desk. Enough. I couldn't continue pretending to be a grammar teacher.

I said, "Why did John go to the store?"

They looked surprised. "Hey, man, what's this? This isn't grammar."

"I'm asking you a simple grammar question. Why did John go to the store? Can't you guess?"

A hand went up. "Yes, Ron?"

"I think John went to the store to get a book on English grammar."

"Why?"

"Because he wanted Mr. McCourt to think he was smart."

"And why did he want Mr. McCourt to think that?"

"Because John has a girlfriend called Rose, and she's a good girl and she understands grammar. She's going to graduate and become a secretary in a big company in Manhattan. John doesn't want to look stupid in front of her because he wants to marry her. That's why he goes to the store. He's going to be a good boy and study his book. When he doesn't understand something, he'll ask Mr. McCourt because Mr. McCourt knows everything.

When John marries Rose, he's going to invite Mr. McCourt to the wedding."

"Thank you, Ron."

There was an explosion of cheering in the class, but Ron hadn't finished. His hand went up again.

"Yes, Ron?"

"When John got to the store, he didn't have any money so he had to steal the grammar book. When he tried to walk out of the store, the police were called and now he's in Sing Sing prison and poor Rose is crying."

"Poor Rose," the class said sadly. The boys wanted to know where she lived. Girls dried their eyes. But Kenny Ball, the class tough guy, said that the story was just a lot of trash. He said, "Teacher writes a sentence on the board, and suddenly a guy steals a book and goes to Sing Sing. It's all trash and this isn't a real English class."

Ron said, "So can you do better?"

"All these stories don't mean anything. They won't help us get a job."

The bell rang and they left.

The next day, Ron put up his hand again. "Hey, teacher, what would happen if you played around with those words?"

"What do you mean?"

"If you wrote, 'To the store John went.' How about that?"

"Same thing. John's still the subject of the sentence."

"OK. What about 'Went John to the store?'"

"Same thing. It still has a meaning. But you could make it meaningless. If you said to someone, 'John store to the went,' they'd think it was gibberish."

"What's gibberish?"

"Language without any meaning."

I had a sudden idea. I said, "Psychology is the study of the way people behave. Grammar is the study of the way language behaves." Go on, teacher man. Write the word on the board. They

19

like big words. They take them home and frighten their families with them.

"*Psychology*. Who knows it?"

"It's when you study crazy people before you put them in a madhouse."

The class laughed. "Yeah. Like this school, man."

I said, "If someone acts crazy, the psychologist studies them to discover what's wrong. If someone *talks* in a funny way and you can't understand them, then you're thinking about grammar. Like, 'John store to the went.'"

"So it's gibberish, right?" I continued.

They liked that word and they wrote it in their notebooks. And I felt proud. They said it to each other and laughed. After teaching for four years, I'd managed to teach them one new word. In ten years' time, they'd hear *gibberish* and think of me. Something was happening. They were beginning to understand what grammar was. If I continued like this, I might understand it myself.

Chapter 7   Excuse Notes

Mikey Dolan gave me a note from his mother explaining his absence the day before:

Dear Mr. McCort, Mikey's grandmother fell down the stairs from too much coffee, and I kept Mikey at home to take care of her and his baby sister. Please excuse Mikey and he'll do his best in the future because he likes your class.

The note had clearly been forged by Mikey, but I said nothing. It was not the first dishonest note I'd received from him. It wouldn't be the last. Most of the excuse notes in my desk drawer were written by the boys and girls of McKee Vocational High

School. If I said anything, it would hurt their feelings and destroy the relationship between teacher and students. Forged excuse notes are just a part of school life. Everyone knows they're fiction, so what's the problem?

I threw Mikey's note into a desk drawer with all the others. While my class was taking a test one day, I read all the notes carefully. I made two piles, one for the real notes, the other for the forged ones. The second pile was larger.

"Isn't it strange," I thought, "how they never like writing in class or for homework? But when they forge these excuse notes, they're wonderful. I have a drawer full of excuse notes that would make an excellent book: *Great American Excuses.*"

Why hadn't I noticed this drawer full of great writing before— this palace of literature, these jewels of fiction, imagination, and self-pity, with details of family problems, kitchen explosions, falling ceilings, sudden deaths, unexpected births, illnesses, robberies, and badly-behaved babies? Here was American high school writing at its best—real, urgent, clear, short, fiction:

The oven caught fire and the fire department kept us out of the house all night.

The toilet was broken so we had to use the toilet in Kilkenny Bar, but that was broken too.

The train door shut on Arnold's homework bag and took it away.

His sister's dog ate the homework and I hope it kills him.

A man died in the bathroom upstairs and the water from the bath came through the ceiling and fell onto Roberta's homework.

Her big brother got mad with her and threw her homework out the window.

I imagined the writers of excuse notes on buses and trains, in coffee shops and on park seats, trying to discover new and believable excuses, trying to write in their parents' style.

They didn't know that honest excuse notes from parents were usually boring.

I typed several of the excuse notes and gave copies to my students. They read silently.

"Hey, Mr. McCourt, what's this?"

"Excuse notes."

"What do you mean? Who wrote them?"

"You did, or some of you did. They're not really from your parents, are they, Mikey?"

"So, what do you want us to do with these excuse notes?"

"Read them to the class. This is the first class in the world to study the art of the excuse note and to practice writing them."

They were smiling. They understood.

"Some of the notes on that sheet were written by people in this class. You know who you are. You used your imagination. You'll need excuses in the future, in the world outside, so you need to make them believable. Try it now. Imagine you have a fifteen-year-old son or daughter who needs an excuse for not doing homework."

They didn't look around. They didn't eat their pens or look bored. They were enthusiastic about writing excuses for their future sons and daughters. It was an act of loyalty and love.

They produced lots of excuses, from food poisoning blamed on the McKee High School cafeteria to a heavy truck crashing into their house.

They said, "More, more. Could we do more?"

I was surprised. I went to the board and wrote: "For Homework Tonight."

That was a mistake. The class complained. They didn't like the word *homework*. I crossed it out and wrote the titles: "An Excuse

Note from Adam to God" or "An Excuse Note from Eve to God." "You can start it now," I said.

Heads went down. Pens raced across paper. Secret smiles around the room. "Oh, this is good," they think, and we know what's coming, don't we? Adam blames Eve. Eve blames Adam. They both blame God, who throws them out of the Garden of Eden. So Adam and Eve and their children's children go to McKee Vocational High School and practice writing excuse notes for the first man and woman. And maybe God Himself needs an excuse note for some of His big mistakes.

The bell rang. For the first time in my four years of teaching, I saw high school students unwilling to leave the classroom.

The next day, everyone had excuse notes from Adam and Eve. Lisa Quinn defended Eve. Eve gave Adam the apple from the Tree of Knowledge because she was bored with life in the Garden of Eden. She was also tired of God watching them all the time. They had no private places. God was lucky. He could hide behind a cloud if He wanted to be private.

There were enthusiastic discussions although no one said anything really bad about God. Maybe, though, He punished the First Man or First Woman a bit too hard.

"Mr. McCourt, the principal is at the door."

My heart sank.

The principal came into the room with the Staten Island Chief Inspector of Schools, Mr. Martin Wolfson. They didn't look at me. They didn't apologize for interrupting my class. They walked up and down, looking at student papers. They picked them up and examined them carefully. The inspector showed one to the principal. The principal looked serious. The class understood that these were important people. They stayed loyal to me and no one asked for the bathroom.

On their way out the principal whispered that the inspector would like to see me after the class. I know. I know. I've done

23

something wrong again. You do your best. You get your class interested in writing. You do something that's never been done before in the history of the world. But now it's judgment time. I went to the principal's office.

He was sitting at his desk. The inspector was standing in the middle of the room.

"Come in. Come in. Only a minute. I want to tell you that your lesson was of the highest quality. That, young man, is what we need. Good quality teaching. Those kids were writing on a college level. Those excuse notes from Adam and Eve were excellent. There are some good future lawyers in that class. So, I just want to shake your hand and congratulate you. There will be a good report about you. Thank you."

Shall I dance back to the classroom or shall I fly? Will the world complain if I sing?

I sang. The next day I taught my class a silly song with difficult pronunciation. They laughed as they tried to get their tongues around the words. And wasn't it great to see the teacher singing? School should be like this every day.

Chapter 8   Kevin

Teachers refuse to have Kevin Dunne in their classes. The kid's a real troublemaker, out of control. If the principal tries to put him in their classes, they'll leave the school. That kid belongs in a zoo, not a school.

So they send him to the new teacher, the one who can't say no: me. Also, you can see with that red hair and his name that the kid's Irish. An Irish teacher with the same accent will be able to manage the little animal. A real Irish teacher can probably touch something deep inside him. The guidance counselor says that Kevin's almost nineteen and has had to repeat two years. But he should graduate this year. The school's hoping that he'll leave the school, join the army or something. The army accepts all kinds of people, even the Kevins of this world. He'll never reach my classroom alone, so would I please collect him from the office?

He sits in an office corner, wearing a coat too big for him and a dark hat. The guidance counselor says, "Here's your new teacher, Kevin. Lift your head so he can see you."

Kevin doesn't move.

"Lift your head, Kevin."

Kevin shakes his head.

"OK. Go with Mr. McCourt and try to behave."

In class, he sits at his desk drumming with his fingers, hiding inside his coat. The principal comes in and tells him, "Son, take off that hat." Kevin pays no attention. The principal turns to me. "Are we having a problem here?"

"That's Kevin Dunne."

"Oh," and he leaves the classroom.

I feel imprisoned in some kind of mystery. When I talk about him to other teachers, they tell me impossible students are always given to the new teachers. The guidance counselor tells me, "Don't worry about it. Kevin's trouble, but there's something wrong with his brain. He won't be here long. Just be patient."

The next day, just before noon, he asks to go to the bathroom. He says, "Why do you let me go so easily? You don't want me here, do you?"

"You wanted my permission. I'm giving it. Go."

"Why are you telling me to go?"

"Because you want to."

"That's not fair. I didn't do anything wrong."

I want to explain things to him quietly, but I'm not good at that. It's easier to talk to the whole class than to one boy. It isn't so personal.

He says strange things in the middle of class: "English has more dirty words than any other language"; "If you wear your right shoe

25

on your left foot and your left shoe on your right foot, your brain will be more powerful and all your children will be twins"; "God has a pen that never needs ink"; "Babies know everything when they're born. That's why they can't talk. If they did, we'd all be stupid." "Beans make you smell. If you feed your children beans, police dogs can find them when they get lost or kidnapped. That's why rich families feed their children a lot of beans." When he left school, he was going to teach dogs how to find rich bean-eating kids. He'd be rich and famous, and could he now go to the bathroom?

His mother visits on Open School Day. She can do nothing with him, doesn't know what's wrong with him. His father ran off when Kevin was four and now lives in Pennsylvania with a woman who sells white mice to scientists. Kevin loves the white mice but hates his father's new wife for selling them to people who cut them open. When he was ten, he attacked the woman and the police were called. Now his mother wonders how he's doing in my class. Is he learning anything?

I tell her he's a smart boy with a good imagination. She says, "Yeah, that's fine for you. But what about his future?" She's worried he'll join the army and be sent to Vietnam. I tell her I don't think they'll take him in the army and she looks offended. She says, "What do you mean? He's as good as any kid in this school."

"I mean I don't think he'd like the army."

"My Kevin can do anything."

His mother loves him, other teachers refuse to have him, and I don't know what to do with him. I try to talk to him, but he pretends not to hear me. I send him to the guidance counselor, who returns him with a note. The counselor advises me to keep him busy. Make him wash the blackboards.

I tell Kevin I'm making him classroom manager in charge of everything. He finishes his jobs quickly to show the class how fast he is. In the closet he finds hundreds of dirty, dry little paint jars. He says, "Oh, man. Jars, jars. Colors, colors. Mine, mine."

"OK, Kevin. Would you like to clean them? You can stay here at this special table and you don't have to sit at your desk."

"Yeah, yeah. My jars. My table. I'm going to take off my hat."

He takes off his hat, and his hair is flame-red. I tell him I've never seen such red hair and he smiles. He works with the jars for hours, cleaning them and arranging them on shelves. At the end of the year he still hasn't finished. I tell him he won't be able to stay during the summer and he cries. Could he take the jars home? His face is wet with tears.

"All right, Kevin. Take them home."

He touches my shoulder with his paint-covered hand and tells me I'm the greatest teacher in the world.

He takes home boxes of glass jars.

He doesn't return in September. He is sent to a special school for unteachable children. He runs away and lives for a short time with the white mice in his father's garage. Then the army takes him, and his mother comes to the school to tell me he's missing in Vietnam. She shows me a picture of his room. On the table the glass jars are arranged into letters that spell MCCORT OK.

"Look," his mother says. "He liked you for helping him, but the Communists got him. So tell me, what's the purpose in that? Can you tell me what's happening over there in a country nobody's heard of? Will you tell me that?"

From a bag she pulls a large jar filled with Kevin's dried paints. She says, "Look at that. All the colors in the world are in that jar. And you know what? He cut off all his hair. You can see where he mixed it in with all those paints. That's a work of art, isn't it? I know he'd want you to have it."

I keep the jar on my desk, where it shines like a light. When I look at it, I feel very sorry for letting him leave school and go to Vietnam.

My students, especially the girls, say the jar is beautiful. A work of art. I tell them about Kevin and some of the girls cry.

A cleaner thinks the jar is a piece of garbage and takes it away to the trash can in the yard.

I talk to teachers in the cafeteria about Kevin. They shake their heads. They say, "That's terrible. We lose some of the kids, but what can we do? We have large classes, no time, and we're not psychologists."

Chapter 9   The College Lecturer

One day, the guidance counselor stopped me outside my classroom.

"What's this about Barbara Sadlar?" he wanted to know.

"What do you mean?"

"She came to my office and said you advised her to go to college."

"That's right."

"I'd like to remind you that this is a vocational high school. These kids go into ordinary jobs, son. They're not ready for college."

I told him Barbara Sadlar was one of the smartest students in my five classes. She wrote well, read books, did well in class discussions. I'd gone to college and become a teacher without any high school education. Why couldn't Barbara? She didn't have to be a secretary or hairdresser if she didn't want to be.

"Because, young man, you're giving kids ideas they shouldn't have. We're trying to prepare them for life in the real world, and you're filling their heads with useless, crazy ideas. I'll have to talk to her now. Why don't you just teach English, and leave guidance counseling to me?"

He started to walk away but turned back again and said, "Is it because she's good-looking?"

I wanted to tell him what I thought of him, but I stayed silent.

A few days later, he left a card for me in my mailbox: "A man should try to carry more than he can hold. But make sure there is something to hold. Don't give your students impossible dreams."

♦

When I was thirty, I married Alberta Small. I also did a one-year higher degree course at Brooklyn College in English Literature. It would help me go up in the world and earn more money.

In 1966, after eight years at McKee, it was time to leave. With my new higher degree, I was going to a college in Brooklyn. A friend, Professor Herbert Miller, had helped me find a job there as a lecturer. I would have five or six classes every week, not every day. I'd earn much less money than a high school teacher, but I'd have more free time. The students would be older, so they'd listen and work harder. Also, they'd call me professor, which would make me feel important. I was going to teach two courses: Introduction to Literature and General Writing.

My students were adult, mostly under thirty, working around the city in stores, factories, and offices. There was a class of thirty-three firefighters, all white, mostly Irish. Almost everyone else was black or Hispanic. There were no problems with classroom behavior, so I had to use different teaching methods.

I had to get up there and teach.

♦

Freddie Bell was a well-dressed young black man who worked in the men's clothing department at the Abraham and Strauss Department Store. He liked to write in a colorful style using big, unusual words from a dictionary. When I wrote on his paper, "Use simpler language," he said, "Why should anyone write like a baby?"

"Because, Freddie, people want to read clear writing, not smart writing."

He didn't agree. His high school English teacher had told him the English language was like a wonderful, powerful musical instrument. Play all the notes loudly.

"But, Freddie, your writing is unnatural and false."

That was the wrong thing to say, especially with thirty other students watching and listening. His face froze, and I knew I'd lost him. This upset me, because I knew there would be a bad feeling in the class.

He hit back at me with language. His writing became more unnatural and false. His grades fell from A to B-. Finally, he asked me to explain. He said he'd shown his work to his old English teacher, who couldn't understand the fall in grades. Look at the language. Look at the vocabulary. Look at the levels of meaning. Look at the complicated sentences.

We stared at each other. He refused to accept my opinion. He said he worked hard in my class, looking up new words. He didn't want to give me the same boring words all the time. His old teacher had told him that there was nothing worse than pages of student writing with no new thoughts or fresh vocabulary. His old teacher thought that I should reward him for trying new things. He also wanted me to know that he worked hard in the department store to pay his way through college.

"I don't see the connection between that and your writing."

"Also, it's not easy when you're black in this society."

"Oh, Freddie, this society isn't easy for anybody. All right. If you want an A, I'll give you an A."

"No, I don't want it just because you're angry or because I'm black. I want it because I deserve it."

I turned to walk away. He called after me, "Hey, Mr. McCourt, thanks. I like your class. It's strange, your class, but maybe I'll become a teacher like you."

◆

Students have to produce a research paper for one of my courses.

They have to show the ability to choose a subject, do simple research, and write cards saying where their material came from. They also have to make a list of the books that they use.

I take my students to the library, where the friendly librarian shows them how to find information and use the necessary tools of research. They listen to her and look at each other and whisper in Spanish and French. But when she asks if they have any questions, they stare silently. This embarrasses the librarian, who's trying to be helpful.

Later, I try to explain the simple idea of research.

"First, you choose a subject."

"What's that?"

"Think of something you're interested in. Maybe a problem that's bothering you and people in general. You could write about money, religion, children, politics, or education. Some of you come from Haiti or Cuba—two very interesting subjects. You could write about the importance of magic in Haiti or the American attack on Cuba. You could research freedom in your country, think about the advantages and disadvantages, make a final decision."

They don't know what I'm talking about so I have to explain it in another way. I ask them their opinions on gun control. They stare at me with an empty look in their eyes. They don't understand. How could they? Nobody ever told them they could have opinions.

The lesson isn't a success.

There are ten minutes before the end of the class. I tell the students to go and look around the library. No one moves. They don't even whisper. They sit in their winter coats. They hold book bags and wait for the end of the class.

After class I tell my friend, Professor Herbert Miller, about my problem. He says, "They work hard days and nights. They come to class. They sit and listen. They do their best. The college lets them in, then expects the teacher to perform magic or be a tough guy. Research? How can these people do research? They have a hard time reading a newspaper."

I am shocked. I didn't realize the people in my classes thought their opinions didn't matter. Whatever ideas they had came from TV and magazines. No one had ever told them they could think for themselves.

I tell them, "You have a duty to think for yourselves."

Silence in the classroom. I say, "You don't have to believe everything I tell you. You can ask questions. If I don't have the answer, we can find it in the library or discuss it here."

They look at each other. Yeah. The man's talking funny. Tells us we don't have to believe him. Hey, we came here to learn English. We've got to graduate.

I want to save them. I want to lift them from their knees after hours of boring work in offices and factories. I want to take them out of prison, lead them to the mountaintop, teach them to breathe the air of freedom.

But life is already difficult enough for these people. They don't need an English teacher talking about freedom of thought and bothering them with questions.

"Man, we just want to pass our examinations."

In the end, the research papers are very bad. Students have copied straight from books. One, Vivian, has mixed English with Haitian French and written more than seventeen pages. I give her paper a B+ for the hard work of reading and copying.

When I return the papers, I try to say positive things about them. I want the students to think about their subjects even more deeply.

I am talking to myself. It is the last class of the year, and they are looking at their watches. I walk to the subway, angry with myself for not doing better with them. Four women from the class are waiting for a train. They smile and ask if I live in Manhattan.

"No. Brooklyn."

I don't know what to say after that. No friendly conversation from the professor.

Vivian says, "Thanks for the grade, Mr. McCourt. That's the highest I ever got in English. And, you know, you're a good teacher."

The others smile. I know they are just being polite. When the train comes, they say, "See you," and hurry away.

Chapter 10   Fashion High School

My college teaching career ended in a year. The college principal said I needed to take more examinations if I wanted to stay. I told him I didn't want to take more examinations.

"Sorry," said the principal.

My wife said I was going nowhere in life. She said, "We've been married for six years, and you just go from one school to another. Soon you'll be forty, and you'll wonder where your life went."

I agreed with her, but I couldn't tell her. I made a speech about life and America. I told her life was an adventure, and maybe I was living in the wrong century. Why couldn't I be alive in the nineteenth century, when men rode horses across deserts and protected their families from enemies and wild animals with guns? I loved that part of American history.

Alberta said, "Go and get a job."

I replied angrily, "A job is death without self-respect."

She said, "You'll have your self-respect, but you won't have me."

You could see there was little hope for the future of that marriage.

◆

The head of the Education Department at Fashion High

School didn't like me, but he needed a teacher urgently. No one wanted to teach in vocational high school, and I had eight years' experience at McKee.

"That's not a very good school, is it?" he said from behind his desk.

I needed that job and didn't want to offend him. I told him I'd learned a lot about teaching at McKee. He said, "We'll see."

It was clear my future was not in this school. I wondered if I had a future anywhere in the school system. He said four teachers in his department were doing management courses. One day, they'd have important jobs in schools around the city.

"We're not lazy here," he said. "We move on and up. What are *your* plans for the future?"

"I don't know. I suppose I just came here to be a teacher," I said.

He shook his head. "Why should you spend all your life in a classroom with kids? Why don't you want to move on and up like those four teachers in my department?"

I suddenly felt brave and asked him, "If everyone moved on and up, who'd teach the children?"

He ignored me, giving a small smile with a mouth that had no lips.

♦

"This is the plastic tube that holds the ink," I said to the class, holding up a ballpoint pen. "If you took away the tube, what would happen?"

The students couldn't believe such a stupid question. "You wouldn't be able to write."

"OK. Now what am I holding in my hand?"

Again the patient look. "That's a spring."

"And what happens when we take away the spring?"

"The tube doesn't write because there's no spring to push it out. Then you get into trouble because you can't write your homework. And the teacher will think you're crazy if you talk about missing springs and tubes."

I wrote on the board: "The spring makes the pen work."

"What's the subject of this sentence? In other words, what are we talking about in this sentence?"

"The pen."

"No, no, no. There's an action word here. It's called a verb. What is it?"

"Oh, yeah. The spring."

"No, no, no. The spring is a thing."

"Yeah, yeah. The spring is a thing. Hey, man. That's a poem."

"So, what does the spring do?"

"It makes the pen work."

"Good. The spring is the subject—it performs the action. We're talking about the spring, aren't we?"

They looked doubtful.

"Would it be right to say, 'The pen makes the spring work'?"

"No. The spring makes the pen work. Even a fool can see that."

"So, what is the action word?"

"*Makes.*"

"Right. And what word uses the action word?"

"*Spring.*"

"So you can see how a ballpoint pen is like a sentence. It needs something to make it work. It needs action, a verb. Can you see that?"

They said they could. The head of the department, making notes in the back of the room, looked puzzled. After the class, he said that the ballpoint pen was a good idea. Maybe the class didn't understand the connection between the pen and a sentence, but I was using my imagination. Of course, some of his more experienced teachers would do it better, but it was a smart idea.

◆

When I pulled my shoelace one morning and it broke, I used bad language.

Alberta asked, "What's the matter?"

"I broke my shoelace."

"You're always breaking shoelaces."

"No, I'm not always breaking shoelaces. I haven't broken a shoelace for years."

"If you didn't pull them so hard, they wouldn't break."

"What are you talking about? The shoelace was two years old. I pulled on it in the same way that you force cupboard drawers."

"I don't force cupboard drawers."

"Yes, you do. When they don't open, you get angry."

"I don't break them."

"No, you just pull them so hard that you can't open them ever again. Then you have to pay a lot of money to get them fixed."

"If we didn't have such cheap furniture, the drawers would be OK. Oh, why didn't I listen to my friends? They warned me not to marry an Irishman."

I never won arguments with my wife. She always changed the subject. She always blamed me for being Irish.

I went to school in a terrible temper, in no mood for teaching or being nice. "Come on, Stan, sit down. Joanna, put your make-up away, please. Are you listening? Open your copy of *Practical English*, page nine. Do the vocabulary questions; then we'll check your answers."

They said, "Yeah, yeah. Keep the teacher happy." They turned the pages slowly. Before they reached page nine, they had to discuss things with their friends in front, behind, beside them. They talked about last night's programs on TV and a girl in another class who was going to have a baby.

"Would you open the magazine to page nine?"

Fifteen minutes later, they still hadn't found page nine. "Hector, open the magazine to page nine."

He had straight black hair and a thin pale face. He ignored me and stared straight ahead.

"Hector, open the magazine."

He shook his head.

I walked toward him holding a copy of the magazine. "Hector, the magazine. Open it."

He shook his head again. I hit him across the face with the magazine. There was a red mark below his eye. He jumped up. "Drop dead," he said, tears in his voice. He walked toward the door, and I called after him, "Sit down, Hector," but he was gone. I wanted to run after him and apologize, but I let him go. When I was calmer, I might be able to talk to him.

I dropped the magazine on my desk and sat there for the rest of the hour, staring ahead like Hector. The class didn't even pretend to find page nine. They watched me quietly, or stared out the window.

Should I talk to them, apologize to them? No, no. Teachers don't apologize for their mistakes. Teachers mustn't be weak. We waited for the bell. When they were leaving the room, Sofia, from the seat next to Hector's, said, "That was wrong. You're a nice man, but Hector's nice, too. He's got a lot of problems, and now you've made them worse."

Now the class was going to hate me, especially the Cubans, Hector's group. There were thirteen Cubans in the class. They believed they were better than the other Spanish-speaking groups. Every Friday they wore white shirts, blue ties and black pants to show the difference between them and the other groups, especially the Puerto Ricans.

It was the middle of September. If I didn't improve my relationship with the Cubans, they'd make my life miserable until the end of the year.

At lunch Melvin, a guidance counselor, sat at my table. "Hi. What happened with you and Hector?"

I told him.

"That's a pity. I wanted him in your class because he had questions about the Irish. You'd be able to answer them. He's also ashamed of his mother. She used to sell herself to men in Havana. And he's got sexual problems himself. He doesn't know whether he likes girls or boys. Now he thinks you hate people like him. He says he's going to hate all the Irish, and his Cuban friends will hate all the Irish. But, he has no Cuban friends. They stay away from him. And his family's ashamed of him."

"Oh, hell. He didn't obey me. He refused to open the magazine. I don't want to be caught in a sex and nationality war."

Melvin asked me to meet with him and Hector in the guidance office.

"Hector, Mr. McCourt wants you and him to understand each other."

"I don't care what Mr. McCourt wants. I don't want an Irish teacher. They drink. They hit people for no reason."

"Hector, you didn't open the magazine when I told you."

He stared at me with cold dark eyes. "You're not a teacher. My mother was a teacher."

"Your mother …" I almost said it, but he was gone. Melvin shook his head, and I knew that my time at Fashion High School was finished. Melvin said that Hector could take me to court for attacking him. If he did, I was in big trouble.

Of course, the head of the department heard about my problem with Hector. He said nothing until the day before the vacation began. Then he put a letter in my mailbox saying there would be no job for me after the vacation.

When I met him in the hall, he said I shouldn't stop trying. I might succeed as a teacher. He'd noticed that sometimes my lessons were very good, especially the one about the ballpoint pen and the sentence.

Chapter 11 The Moon in the Lake

Alberta says they're looking for a teacher at her high school, Seward Park on the Lower East Side. There are students from all kinds of backgrounds in this school: Jewish, Chinese, Puerto Rican, Greek, Dominican, Russian, Italian. I've had no training for teaching English as a Second Language. These students don't want to know about English literature, they want to speak the language. If you can't speak English, you'll look stupid and you won't make new friends.

The bell rings and I can hear many different languages in my class.

"Excuse me."

They ignore me or they don't understand my polite request.

Again. "Excuse me."

A big red-haired Dominican boy called Oscar catches my eye. "Teacher, you want help?"

He climbs up on his desk and everyone cheers because this is against the rules.

"Hey," Oscar shouts. "Be quiet. Listen to the teacher."

"Thanks, Oscar, but would you please climb down?"

"So, mister, what's your name?"

I write on the board, MR. McCOURT.

"Hey, mister, you Jewish?'

"No."

"All the teachers here are Jewish. Why aren't you?"

"I don't know."

The class is shocked into silence. What? The teacher doesn't know? Maybe this teacher man's human like us?

A few years ago I was the same as them, recently arrived in America and the bottom of the social ladder. Even now, although I know English, I understand their fears and confusions. I could easily sit down with them, ask them about their families, tell them about myself. I want to lock the door and shut out the world until they speak enough English to get a girl.

I look at this collection of kids from all continents, faces of all colors and shapes: Asians with black hair and eyes; the great brown eyes of Hispanic boys and girls; the shyness of some, the loudness of others. I feel at home with them all.

◆

Nancy Chu asks if she can talk to me after class. She sits at her desk and waits for the room to be empty.

"I'm here three years, from China."

"Your English is very good, Nancy."

"Thank you. I learned English from Fred Astaire."

"Fred Astaire?"

"I know all the songs from his movies. My favorite is *Top Hat*. I sing his songs all the time. My parents think I'm crazy. My friends, too. I have trouble with my parents all the time because of Fred Astaire."

"Well, it's unusual, Nancy."

"Also, I watch you teach. And I wonder why you're so nervous. You know English, so you should be relaxed. The kids all say, if they knew English they'd be so relaxed. Sometimes you're not nervous, and the kids like that. They like it when you tell stories and sing. When I'm nervous, I sing 'Dancing in the Dark'. You should learn that, Mr. McCourt, and sing it to the class. You don't have such a bad voice."

"Nancy, I'm an English teacher. I'm not a song-and-dance man."

"Could you tell me how to be an English teacher?"

"But what will your parents say?"

"They think I'm crazy already. They say they're sorry they ever brought me from China, where there's no Fred Astaire. They say I'm not even Chinese now. They think it's a waste of time to be a teacher and to listen to Fred Astaire. 'You come here to make money,' my parents say. Mr. McCourt, will you tell me how to be an English teacher?"

"I will, Nancy."

The next day in class, Nancy Chu says, "You were lucky you knew English when you came to America. How did you feel when you came to America?"

"Confused. Do you know what *confused* means?"

The word goes around the room. They explain it to each other in their own languages. They're surprised their teacher was as confused as they are now.

I tell them I had trouble with language and the names of things when I came to New York. I didn't even know what a hot dog was.

Nancy dreams of taking her mother to a Fred Astaire movie because her mother never goes out and she's a very intelligent woman. Her mother knows many Chinese poems, especially poems by Li Po. "Have you ever heard of Li Po, Mr. McCourt?"

"No."

She tells the class her mother loves Li Po because he died in a beautiful way. One bright moonlit night, he drank rice wine and took his boat out on a lake. He could see the moon in the water and thought it looked so beautiful. When he reached out to touch it, he fell into the lake and died.

Nancy's mother dreamed of going back to China and taking a boat out on the same lake. If she got very old or had a serious illness, she wanted to reach over the side of the boat and touch the moon in the water. Nancy has tears in her eyes when she tells us this.

When the bell rings, the students don't jump from their seats. They take their things and leave the classroom quietly. I'm sure they all have pictures of moons and lakes in their heads.

Chapter 12   A Trip to the Movies

In 1968, at Seward Park High School, I had five classes: three English as a Second Language classes and two regular ninth-grade English classes. In one of those ninth-grade classes, there were twenty-nine girls.

The girls ignored me, a white guy standing up there trying to get their attention. They had stuff to talk about. There was always an adventure from last night. Boys. Boys. Boys. Serena said she didn't go out with boys. She went out with *men*. She had red hair, coffee-colored skin, and was so thin that tight clothes hung loose on her. She was fifteen and the center of the class.

The class complained to me. "We don't do anything in this class. Other classes do interesting things. Why don't we?"

I brought in a tape recorder. I was sure they'd like to hear themselves talking. Serena took the microphone.

"My sister was taken away by the police last night. My sister's a nice person. She only took two pieces of meat from a store. White people take things all the time, but the police don't stop *them*. I've seen white women walk out of the store with whole chickens under their dresses. Now my sister's in prison until she goes to court."

She stopped, looked at me for the first time and gave me the microphone. "I don't know why I'm telling you this. You're just a teacher. You're just a white man." She turned away and walked to her seat.

For the first time that year the room was quiet. They waited for me to speak, but I couldn't think of anything to say.

"Anyone else?" I finally asked.

They stared at me silently. Then a hand went up. It was Maria, a smart well-dressed girl who kept a well-ordered notebook. She had a question.

"Other classes go to the movies. Why can't we go to the movies?"

The class cheered their agreement with her.

"OK," I agreed.

The next day, they brought me notes from their parents giving them permission to take a trip to see a movie. About twelve of the notes were forged.

On the six-block walk to the subway, the group of twenty-nine black girls and one white teacher received a lot of attention. The kids ran into stores to buy candy, hot dogs, and bottles of pink drink.

Down the steps, into the subway. They ran through the gates as ticket collectors shouted at them. I walked slowly, pretending I wasn't with them.

They ran backwards and forwards, impatient for the train. They pretended to push each other onto the line. "Teacher, teacher, she tried to kill me. Did you see that?"

People waiting for the train stared angrily at me. A man said, "Why don't they go back where they belong? They don't know how to behave like humans."

I wanted to be brave and defend my twenty-nine noisy girls. You try it, Mister Angry Citizen. You try taking twenty-nine girls on the subway, all excited about being fifteen and escaping from school for a day, all filled with sugar from cookies, candy, and pink drinks. Try teaching them every day while they look at you like you're a white snowman in the sun.

I said nothing and hoped the train would arrive soon.

On the train they screamed and pushed and fought for seats. The passengers looked unfriendly. "Why aren't these kids in school? I'm not surprised they're so stupid."

At West Fourth Street a fat white woman got on the train. The girls stared at her and laughed. She stared back. "What are you looking at?"

Serena said, "We've never seen a mountain get on a train before."

The other twenty-eight girls laughed. Serena stared, unsmiling, at the large woman, who said, "Come here and I'll show you how a mountain can move."

I was the teacher. I had to do something, but what? Then I had a strange feeling. I looked at the other passengers with their unfriendly, angry faces, and I wanted to defend my twenty-nine students.

I stood with my back to the large woman to stop Serena from getting near her.

The girls called, "Get her, Serena! Get her!"

The train pulled into the Fourteenth Street station, and the large woman got out. "You're lucky I have to get off here," she said to Serena, "or I'd eat you for breakfast."

Serena stared at her. "Yeah, fat woman, you really need breakfast."

I moved in front of Serena to stop her from following the woman off the train. She looked at me in a way that was satisfying but puzzling. If I could win her support, the class would be with me. They'd say, "That's Mr. McCourt, the teacher who stopped Serena from getting into a fight with a white woman on the train. He's on our side. He's OK."

Along Forty-second Street, toward Times Square, Maria walked beside me. She said, "You know, we've never been to Times Square before."

I wanted to hug her for talking to me. Instead I said, "You should come here at night to see the lights."

At the theater they rushed to the ticket office, pushing each other out of the way. Five stayed near me, giving me embarrassed looks.

"What's the matter? Aren't you getting tickets?" I asked.

They looked away and said they had no money. I thought of saying, "Well, why the hell did you come here?" but I didn't want to spoil my new, good relationship with them.

I bought the tickets, hoping there might be a friendly look or a thank you. Nothing. They took the tickets and ran straight to a store. They'd lied about having no money. They went into the theater with candy and bottles of drink.

I followed them inside, where they pushed and fought for seats, bothering the other customers. A woman complained to me. I asked the girls to sit down and be quiet.

They ignored me. They threw candy at each other and shouted loudly, "Hey, when are we going to see the movie?"

The woman warned me that she might have to call the manager.

I said, "Yes, I want to be here when the manager comes. I want to see what the manager does with them."

The lights went down, the movie started, and my twenty-nine girls became silent. When it ended and the lights came on, no one moved.

"All right," I said. "Let's go. It's finished."

"We know it's finished. We're not blind."

"We have to go home now."

They said they were going to see the movie again.

I told them I was leaving.

"OK, you're leaving."

They stayed to watch the movie for a second time.

Chapter 13   *Hamlet*

The following week a note in my mailbox advertised a trip for our students to see a performance of Hamlet at a college on Long Island. I threw it into the wastepaper basket. Hamlet would be wasted on this class, I thought.

The next day, there were questions.

"Why are the other classes going on a trip to see a play?"

"Well, it's a play by Shakespeare."

"So?"

I said it was a hard play to understand. I didn't think they'd like it.

"Oh, yeah? So what's it about?"

"It's called *Hamlet*. A prince comes home to discover that his father is dead and his mother's already married to his father's brother. Hamlet's angry because he thinks his uncle murdered his father."

The idea interested them.

Serena said, "So why aren't we going to see this play? Is it because the prince is white?"

"All right. I'll see if we can go with the other classes."

A few days later, I took the girls to see the play. As usual, they pushed and fought each other for seats. They laughed and joked a bit during the play, but they didn't behave too badly.

The next day in class Claudia wanted to know, "Why's everybody mean to the girl?"

"Ophelia?"

"Yeah, everybody's mean to her and she's not even black. Why? Nobody tries to push that Hamlet guy in the river. He's a prince but he's unkind to his mother. Why doesn't she get up and hit him across the face?"

Serena, the smart one, put her hand up like an ordinary girl in an ordinary class. I stared at the hand. I was sure she was going to ask for the bathroom. She said, "Hamlet's mom is a queen. Queens don't hit their children like other people. Queens have to act different."

She gave me a straight, confident look. Eyes wide and beautiful, a small smile. This thin, black fifteen-year-old knew her power. I felt my face going red, and all the girls started laughing.

♦

The following Monday, Serena doesn't return to class. The girls say she's never coming back because her mother's gone to prison for drugs and stuff. Now Serena has to live with her grandmother in Georgia, where white people are mean to black people. They say Serena will never stay there. She'll soon get into trouble.

A month after Serena leaves, Maria puts up her hand. "Mr. McCourt, I got a letter from Serena. She said it's her first ever letter, and her grandmother made her write it. She never met her grandmother before, but she loves her because the old lady can't read or write, and Serena reads the Bible to her every night. And you'll like this, Mr. McCourt. She said she's going to finish high school and go to college to teach little kids. Not big kids like us because we're not polite. She wants me to tell you she's sorry about the things she did in class. One day she's going to write you a letter."

Fires of happiness burn inside me. I've never felt so good.

Chapter 14   Andrew and the Tilting Chair

There's a difficult student in every class. He usually sits at the back, where he can tilt his chair against the wall. You've already told the class about the dangers of tilting. "The chair could fall, children, and you could be hurt. Then teacher will have to write a report to stop parents from complaining."

Andrew knows the tilting chair will make you angry. Then he can play the little game that will catch the eyes of the girls. You'll say, "Hey, Andrew."

He won't answer immediately. He'll wait for the girls to look at him.

"What?"

"The chair, Andrew. Would you put it down, please?"

"I'm not doing anything."

"The chair, Andrew, has four legs. Tilting could cause an accident."

Silence in the classroom. This time you feel confident. Andrew is disliked by the group, and he knows he'll get no support from them. He's a pale, thin figure, a lonely boy. But the class is watching him with interest. They may not like him, but they won't like it if the teacher's unkind to him. When it's boy against teacher, they always support the boy.

So, teacher man, what's the problem? Simple. Andrew has shown his dislike for you from day one and you don't like being disliked.

He waits. The class waits. The chair's still tilting. I'd love to take one of its legs and pull. His head would hit the wall and everyone would laugh.

I turn away from Andrew. I don't know why I'm turning away and walking to the front of the room. I really don't know what I'll do or say when I reach my desk. I don't want them to think I've lost. I know I have to act. Andrew's head rests against the wall, and he's giving me a small, unpleasant smile.

I don't like Andrew's long, red hair, or his thin face. Sometimes, when the lesson's going well, I see his cold, unfriendly stare. Should I try to win his support, or should I destroy him completely?

A voice in my head tells me, "Turn the situation to your advantage. Pretend you planned the whole thing." And I say to the class, "So, what's happening here?" They stare. They're puzzled.

I say, "Imagine you're a newspaper reporter. You walked into this room a few minutes ago. What did you see? What did you hear? What's the story?"

Michael puts his hand up. "No story. Just Andrew being stupid as usual."

Andrew loses his little smile and I feel I'm winning. I won't have to say much. Continue with the questions and let the class attack him. I'll take that smile off his face and he'll never tilt again.

I play the part of the calm, patient teacher. "That sentence, Michael, doesn't give the reader much information."

"Yeah, but who needs information like that? Is some guy from the *Daily News* going to walk in here and write a big story about Andrew and the chair and the angry teacher?"

His girlfriend puts her hand up.

"Yes, Diane?"

"I'm going to tell Andrew to put his chair down."

She's sixteen, tall and calm. She reminds me of a Scandinavian actress with her long, yellow hair hanging down her back. I'm nervous when she walks to the back of the room and stands in front of Andrew.

"What's going on inside your head, Andrew? You're wasting everybody's time, so what's your problem? The teacher's getting paid to teach us. He's not paid to tell you to put your chair down. Right, Andrew?"

He's still tilting but he's looking at me with a question in his eyes: "What should I do?"

He tilts his chair forward until it's flat. He stands and looks at Diane. His thoughts are clear: "See? You'll never forget me, Diane. You'll forget this whole class; you'll forget the teacher. But I tilt my chair, the teacher gets angry, and everyone in this class will remember me forever. Right, Mr. McCourt?"

I want to say what I'm really thinking: "Listen, you little fool, put the chair down or I'll throw you out the window." But you can't talk like that. You'd be reported to the principal. You know your job. If they make you angry, you have to suffer in silence. No one's forcing you to stay in this miserable, badly-paid job. If you want to leave, no one will stop you. But stop dreaming. Get back to work. Talk to your class. The problem of the tilting chair's not finished yet. The class is waiting.

"Are you listening?" They smile. "You saw what happened in this room. So you have material for a story, don't you? We've had a problem, Andrew against the teacher. Andrew against the class. Andrew against himself. You were watching, weren't you? What were you thinking? Why's the teacher getting so angry? Or, why's Andrew behaving so stupidly? If you were reporting this, you'd have to think about a third thing. Why was Andrew doing this? Only Andrew knows why he was tilting his chair. You can guess his reasons if you want to. I think we could make about thirty guesses."

The next day, Andrew stays in the classroom after the class. "Mr. McCourt, you went to New York University, didn't you?"

"I did."

"Well, my mother said she knew you."

"Really? I'm happy to know that someone remembered me."

"I mean, she knew you outside of class."

"Really?"

"She died last year. Her name was June."

Oh, God! How could I be so slow? Why didn't I guess? Why didn't I see her in his eyes?

"She often wanted to call you, but she had a bad time with my father and her illness. She made me promise never to tell you about her. She said you probably wouldn't want to talk to her."

But I did want to talk to her. I wanted to talk to her forever. "Who did she marry? Who's your father?"

"I don't know who my father is. She married Gus Peterson. I have to go and pack my things. My dad's moving to Chicago and I'm going with him and his new wife."

We shake hands and I watch him walk down the hallway. Before he disappears, he turns and waves. I wonder for a second whether I should let the past go so easily.

Chapter 15   A Failed Everything

This is the situation in the public schools of America: the farther you travel from the classroom, the greater your financial and professional rewards are. Get your license and teach for two or three years. After you take courses in management and careers guidance, you can move to an office with private toilets, long lunches, and secretaries. You won't have to work with difficult kids all day. If you hide in your office, you won't even have to see them.

But here I was, thirty-eight years old, not wanting to climb in the school system but not wanting to stay where I was. I had other problems, too. My marriage was in trouble. Alberta said I was impossible to live with because I was filled with anger about my childhood. We had violent fights. My life was going wrong, and I thought there was no escape. What could I do?

My wife made a suggestion. "Why don't you do a doctorate in English and go up in the world?"

"I will," I decided.

New York University accepted me, but my wife advised me to go to London or Dublin.

"Do you want me to leave?" I joked.

She smiled.

Trinity College, Dublin, accepted me. I kissed my wife goodbye and sailed to Ireland on the *Queen Elizabeth*. It was the ship's second last trip across the Atlantic. I stayed in Dublin for two years, but it wasn't a success. I was homesick and I drank too much. I also realized, too late, that I'd chosen the wrong research subject for my doctorate. I went for long walks around the city, up one street and down the other. I met a woman who fell in love with me. I didn't know why. I thought about New York—the schools, the bars, the friends—and I wanted to go home.

In January 1971 I returned to New York without a doctorate.

Alberta was going to have a baby—the result of a vacation together the summer before. I pretended to continue with my studies, but I wasn't serious. When Alberta left her teaching job at Seward Park High School to have our baby, I taught there instead of her. A month after I started there, the principal died of a heart attack. Then I met the new principal in the elevator. I'd met him before. He was the man who had, years earlier, asked me to leave Fashion High School. I said, "Are you following me?" He didn't smile. A few weeks later, I lost my job.

I was a failed everything. I looked for my place in the world. I became a substitute teacher, moving from school to school. Students ignored me, and there was nothing I could do. I didn't care if students came to class or not. Principals looked displeased when they saw me sitting at a desk in an almost empty classroom, reading a newspaper. They said I should be teaching. "I'd gladly teach," I replied. "But this is a science class and my subject is English." They knew it was a silly question, but they had to ask. It was their job: "Where are the kids?"

Everyone in school knew the rule. When you see a substitute teacher, run, baby, run.

Chapter 16   Stuyvesant High School

A year after I returned from Dublin, an old friend introduced me to Roger Goodman, the head of the English Department at Stuyvesant High School. He asked me if I'd be interested in teaching there for a couple of months. Stuyvesant was said to be the top high school in the city. If you studied at Stuyvesant, doors opened to the best universities in the country. Every year, thirteen thousand children tried to get in. Only seven hundred succeeded.

After two months, Roger Goodman asked me to stay longer. I accepted, but I promised myself that it was only for two years.

Teachers all over the city wanted jobs at Stuyvesant High School, but I wanted to be out in the world. I wanted to be doing something adult and important. I wanted to have a secretary, fly to important meetings, drink in fashionable bars, go to bed with beautiful women …

When my daughter was born, these dreams disappeared. Her sweet reality was more important than anything else, and I began to feel at home in the world. Every morning, after giving Maggie her bottle, I took the train from Brooklyn to Manhattan. From there, I walked along Fifteenth Street to Stuyvesant, went up to my classroom, and relaxed for a few minutes, looking at the empty desks and thinking of my daughter.

♦

If you asked the boys and girls of Stuyvesant High School to write three hundred fifty words on any subject, they'd write five hundred. If you gave all the students in your five classes written homework just once a week, you'd have to read 43,750 words. If you spent five minutes on each paper, you'd be grading homework for fourteen and a half hours a week. That's how I spent every weekend.

Every day I carried home books and papers in my old, brown bag. The bag sat on the floor in a corner by the kitchen, like a dog waiting for my attention. I didn't want to hide it in a closet because I might forget to read and correct the homework.

I couldn't do it before dinner, so I waited until later. I helped with the dishes, put my daughter to bed. Now, get that bag, man. Sit on the couch, listen to some music, relax for a minute. Close your eyes … suddenly you wake up. There are papers on the floor. You must start work. Look at the first paper. Well-written. Organized. Bitter. This girl's writing about her mother's new husband. He invites her to movies and dinner when her mother works late. Her mother says, "Oh, that's nice." But he looks at

53

her strangely. There's something frightening about his eyes, and then the silence. The writer wonders what she should do. Is she asking me, the teacher? Should I do something? Should I help her with her problem, if there is a problem? She might be inventing it. If I said something to her, what would happen if her mother or her mother's husband heard? No, I should grade her paper and congratulate the writer on her organization and good use of vocabulary. There are some spelling mistakes, but I give her a good grade. "This is good work, Janice. I hope to see more of it next week."

♦

In 1974, my third year at Stuyvesant, I'm invited to be the new Creative Writing teacher. I know nothing about writing or how to teach it. Roger Goodman says, "Don't worry. There are hundreds of creative writing teachers who have never written a book."

I have the usual five classes a day, three "regular" English, two Creative Writing. There are thirty-seven students in my first class. They complain when I say we're going to read *A Tale of Two Cities*. "Why can't we read *The Lord of the Rings*, or a science fiction book? Why can't we …?"

"Enough." I tell them about French history in the 1790s. I talk about the cruel, rich king and the poor, suffering people. I'm on the side of the poor people, and I enjoy getting angry about the unfairness of life. "Even today," I say, "there are many millions of people with no comfortable beds, no hot water, no soap, no warm, white bathrooms."

The students listen politely, but I know they're bored.

"You'll go home to your comfortable apartments and houses," I continue, "and go straight to the refrigerator. It will be full of food, but nothing inside it will please you. You'll ask Mom if you can send out for a pizza. She'll say, 'Of course you can. You have a hard life, learning about poor people in France every day at school. You deserve a little reward.'"

The students stare patiently. Do they know I'm enjoying myself with this long, angry speech? It isn't their fault if they are middle-class and comfortable. To them, I am just another boring old teacher. I am following the old Irish tradition of complaining bitterly about everything.

In front of me, Sylvia puts her hand up. "Calm down, Mr. McCourt. Relax. Where's that big Irish smile?"

I start to say that there is nothing funny about the suffering of poor people in France in the 1790s, but there is an explosion of laughter in the class. Sylvia smiles up at me, and I feel weak and foolish. I sit down and let them joke for the rest of the hour. When the class ends, Ben Chan stays behind. "Mr. McCourt, could I talk to you?"

He knows what I was saying about poor people. The kids in this class don't understand anything. But it isn't their fault, and I shouldn't get angry. He is twelve, but he came to this country four years ago. He knew no English, but he studied hard and learned enough English to pass the Stuyvesant High School entrance examination. He is happy to be here, and his whole family is so proud of him. He beat fourteen thousand kids to get into this school. His father works six days a week, twelve hours a day, in a restaurant in Chinatown. His mother works in a small factory. Every night she cooks dinner for the whole family—five children, her husband, herself. Then she helps get their clothes ready for the next day. She makes sure the children sit at the kitchen table and do their homework. His parents learn English words every day so they can talk to the teachers. Ben says everybody in his family respects each other. No one in his family would ever laugh about poor people in France. They are the same as poor people in China or even in Chinatown, here in New York.

I tell him the story of his family was wonderful. I advise him to write it down and read it to the class.

"Oh, no, I could never do that. Never."

"Why not? The other kids in the class would learn something important about life."

He says, no, he could never write or talk to anyone else about his family. His father and mother would be ashamed.

"Ben, thank you for telling me about your family."

"Oh, I told you because I didn't want you to feel bad after that class."

"Thanks, Ben."

"Thank you, Mr. McCourt. And don't worry about Sylvia. She really likes you."

♦

When my marriage ended, I was forty-nine. Maggie was eight. Teaching forced me to forget my problems. I could cry into my beer in the evening, but in the classroom I had to think about my work. Soon, I could borrow some money for an apartment from a teachers' organization. Until then, Yonk Kling, an artist in his mid-sixties, invited me to stay in his apartment on Hicks Street near Atlantic Avenue.

♦

My Creative Writing classes were so popular with the students that there were never enough chairs for them. Why were the students so enthusiastic? Was it my excellent teaching, my wonderful personality, my Irish humor? Did the boys and girls suddenly want to discuss great things?

Or was it because they knew that my classes were so easy? "McCourt just talks all the time, then gives everyone high grades?"

Although the students were afraid of other teachers, they respected them. They worked hard and they deserved their good grades. But in my classes they were confused. I asked them lots of questions: Why was Hamlet unkind to his mother? Why didn't he kill the king when he had the chance? But I never gave them any answers. "This is America, not Ireland. We like answers here. Or maybe he doesn't know the answers himself."

I wanted to be respected as a serious teacher. I didn't want to be popular only because my class was so easy. "Oh, McCourt's class is garbage. Talk, talk, talk. If you don't get a grade A in his class, you must be stupid."

I joined Yonk one afternoon at a waterfront bar on Atlantic Avenue. He told me I looked terrible.

"Thanks, Yonk."

"Have some wine."

"Just one glass. I have a million papers to correct."

I told Yonk about my problem. "I'm too easy. People don't respect easy teachers. I want to make them earn their grades. Have respect. Hundreds of them want my classes, and that bothers me. One mother begged me to let her daughter into my class. She even invited me to spend the weekend with her. I said no."

Yonk shook his head and said that sometimes I was not very smart. If I didn't relax a bit, I'd soon become a miserable old man. I should learn to spread a little happiness. "A weekend with the mother, a bright writing future for her little girl. What's the matter with you?"

"There wouldn't be any respect."

"Oh, never mind respect. Have another glass of wine."

Chapter 17   The Dinner Conversation

Before Stuyvesant, it was my job to stop students from behaving badly. There, there was no noisy behavior. No flying sandwiches. No pushing or shouting. No excuses for not teaching. If you didn't perform, you'd lose their respect.

The students never stopped trying to get me away from traditional English, but I knew their tricks. I still told stories, but I was learning to connect them to characters in literature. I was finding my voice and my style of teaching. I was learning to be comfortable in the classroom. And at Stuyvesant, I was free to use whatever teaching methods I wanted.

I gave them lessons on music and food. If they complained about studying serious poems, I sang them children's songs or talked about children's stories. Soon, the ideas from these songs and stories were connected to more complicated ideas by more serious writers. The method seemed to work. The students didn't realize they were studying. They thought they were just talking about life.

Whenever a lesson got boring and students began asking for the bathroom, I started a conversation about dinner.

"James, what did you have for dinner last night?"

"Chicken."

"Where did it come from?"

"What do you mean?'

"Did someone buy it, James, or did it fly in the window?"

"My mother bought it."

"So your mother does the shopping?"

"Well, yeah."

"Does she work?"

"Yeah, she's a legal secretary."

"Who cooks the chicken?"

"My mother."

"And what are you doing while your mother's in the kitchen?"

"I'm in my room."

"Doing what?"

"Homework, or listening to music."

"And what's your father doing?"

"Watching the news on TV."

"Who helps your mother in the kitchen?"

"Mr. McCourt, I don't know why you're asking me all these questions. They're so boring."

I turned to the class. "What do you think? This is a writing class. Did you learn anything about James and his family? Is there a story here? Jessica?"

"My mom would never accept that sort of behavior. James and his dad get royal treatment. I'd like to know who washes the dishes. No, I don't have to ask. It's the mom."

I was enjoying myself, and turned to Daniel.

"Daniel, what did you have for dinner last night."

"French-style chicken with baby potatoes and Italian wine."

"Did your mother cook the meal?"

"No, the servant did."

"Oh, the servant. And what was your mother doing?"

"She was with my father."

"So the servant cooked the dinner and served it?"

"That's right."

"And you ate alone?"

"Yes."

"On a shining table of expensive wood, I suppose?"

"That's right."

"Did you have music in the background?"

"Yes. I listened to Telemann for twenty minutes. He's one of my father's favorites. When it ended, I called my father."

"And where was he?"

"He's in Sloan-Kettering hospital. My mother's with him all the time because he's dying."

"Oh, Daniel, I'm sorry. Why didn't you tell me? I was wrong to ask you all those questions."

"It doesn't matter. He's going to die whatever we say."

It was quiet in the classroom. What could I say now to Daniel? I'd played my little game. I'd been a smart, funny teacher, and

Daniel had been patient. Details of his lonely dinner filled the classroom. His father was here. We waited by a bed with Daniel's mother. We'd remember forever the French-style chicken, the servant, and Daniel alone at the shining, expensive table while his father was dying.

Chapter 18   Problems with Parents

On Open School Day, the kids are sent home at noon and the parents come in from one o'clock to three o'clock, and again in the evening from seven o'clock to nine o'clock. At the end of the day, teachers are tired from talking to hundreds of parents. There are three thousand kids in the school, and that should add up to six thousand parents. But this is New York, where almost half the parents are separated. So, there might be ten thousand adults— moms and dads with their new partners. All of them are sure that their children are the smartest in the world. They expect great things for their children, and only total success will satisfy them.

Stanley's parents have separated, and they don't like each other. I'm not surprised Stanley has emotional problems. The mother lives in a large, six-room apartment on the Upper West Side. Dad is in a small, dirty apartment in the Bronx. Stanley spends half the week with his mom and half with his dad, but he's good-humored about it. He's good at math, and he thinks of his life as a mathematical problem. If $a = 3\frac{1}{2}$ and $b = 3\frac{1}{2}$, then what is Stanley?

My monitor on Open School Night is Maureen McSherry. She tells me that Stanley's mother and father are waiting to see me. And, Maureen adds, there are six more couples who refuse to sit next to each other, all fighting and wanting to talk to me.

Stanley's mother, Rhonda, smells of tobacco. She tells me not to believe anything that Stanley's father tells me. She feels sorry for Stanley because he has such a terrible father. "How's Stanley doing at school?"

"Oh, fine. He's a good writer and popular with the other kids."

"Well, that's a surprise, with such a stupid father. I do my best with Stanley when he's with me. But he gets so upset about having to spend three and a half days a week with his father. He's started staying out at night. He says he's staying with friends, but I don't believe him. I know he's got a girlfriend whose parents don't care what they do."

"I'm afraid I don't know anything about that. I'm just his teacher, and it's impossible to get into the private lives of one hundred seventy-five kids."

A few minutes later, I am talking to Stanley's dad, Ben. He says, "I heard what she said." He laughs and shakes his head. "But let's not talk about her. I have this problem with Stanley now. I've spent all this money on his education, and do you know what he wants to do? He wants to go to New England and study the guitar. Tell me, how much money can you earn playing the guitar? I told him I wouldn't let him. We agreed from day one that he was going to work in the financial world. There was never any doubt about that. I mean, what am I working for? A guitar player? No, sir. 'Get your degree and play your guitar in your free time,' I tell him. He cries. He says he's going to live with his mother. I wouldn't want my worst enemy to do that. So, I wonder if you could speak to him? I know he likes your class, talking about food and whatever else you do here."

"I'd like to help, but I'm not a guidance counselor. I'm an English teacher."

"OK, it doesn't matter. Tell me, how's he doing?"

"He's doing well."

The bell rings and Maureen, who's not shy, says that there's no more time. She'd be glad to take names and phone numbers of anyone who wants to meet me another day. She passes around a sheet of paper, which no one writes on. They want my attention here and now. They've waited half the night while these other crazy people talked about their problem kids. Of course the kids have problems—look at the parents. They follow me angrily along the hall, asking how Adam's doing, Sergei, Juan, Naomi? What sort of school is this where you can't even talk to the teacher for a minute? What are we paying taxes for?

At nine o'clock, the teachers leave and go for a drink. We sit at a table in the back of the local bar and order large glasses of beer. Our mouths are dry from talking all night. I tell the other teachers that in all my years at Stuyvesant, only one parent, a mother, has ever asked me if her son was enjoying school. I said, yes, he seemed to be enjoying himself. She smiled, stood up, said, "Thank you," and left. One parent in all those years.

"They only care about success and money, money, money," says Connie, another teacher. "They have high hopes for their kids. We're like workers in a factory. Our job is get their children ready to perform for parent and employer."

A group of parents comes into the bar. One comes over to me. "This is nice," she said. "You have time to drink beer but no time for a parent who waited half an hour to see you."

I tell her I'm sorry.

She angrily joins her group at another table. I feel so tired that I drink too much and stay in bed the next morning. Why didn't I just tell that mother to go to hell?

Chapter 19   Bob and Ken

In my class, Bob Stein never sat at a desk. Maybe he was too big for it, but he liked to sit in the window seat at the back of the room. When he was comfortable, he smiled and waved. "Good morning, Mr. McCourt. Isn't this a great day?"

He wore the same clothes all year: a white shirt open at the neck, a gray jacket, short pants, thick gray socks, and yellow builders' boots. He carried no bag, no books, no notebooks, no pen. He joked that it was my fault because I'd once talked excitedly about Thoreau. The simple life was best, I'd said. Everyone should throw away what they owned.

When I gave the class written work, he always asked to borrow a pen and some paper.

"Bob, this is a writing class. You need a pen and paper."

He told me not to worry. Snow was appearing on my head, he said. I should enjoy my last few years of life.

The class laughed, but he told them he wasn't joking. In a year's time, he said, I'd look back at this minute. And I'd wonder why I wasted my time and emotions on the absence of his pen and paper.

I had to play the part of serious teacher. "Bob, you could fail this class if you don't do the work."

"Mr. McCourt, I can't believe you're telling me this, with your miserable childhood in Ireland and everything. But it's OK. If you fail me, I'll take the course again. No big hurry. Another year or two won't matter. For you, maybe, but I'm only seventeen. I have all the time in the world."

He asked the class if anyone could lend him pen and paper. There were ten offers, but he took them from Jonathan Greenberg, who was sitting nearest him. He didn't want to climb down from his window seat. He said, "You see how nice people are, Mr. McCourt? If other people carry big bags with them, you and I will never have to worry about supplies."

"Yes, Bob. But that won't help you next week when we have the big test on *Gilgamesh*."

"What's that, Mr. McCourt?"

"It's the world-literature book."

"Oh, yeah, I remember that book. Big book. I have it at home, and my dad's reading the bits about the Bible. My dad's a Jewish leader, you know. He was so happy you gave us that book. He said you must be a great teacher. I told him you were a great teacher except you worry too much about pens and paper."

"That's enough, Bob. You haven't even looked at the book."

He told me again not to worry because his father often talked about the book. He, Bob, would find out all about *Gilgamesh* before the big test.

"Bob," I called across the sound of the class laughing. "It would make me happier if you read the book yourself."

"I'd love to, but it doesn't fit into my plans."

"And what are your plans, Bob?"

"I'm going to be a farmer."

He smiled, waved his pen and paper, and apologized for causing trouble in the class. He, Bob, was ready to work. He suggested that the others in the class should do the same. But before we started work, he'd like to explain that he didn't hate world literature. He just liked to read farming magazines. Farming was more complicated than most people realized.

Jonathan Greenberg put up his hand and asked why farming was so complicated.

Bob looked miserable for a second. "It's my dad. I told him I wanted to be a pig farmer. I like pigs. I'm not planning to eat them, but I'd like to farm them and sell them. What's wrong with that? They're really pleasant little animals and they can be very friendly. I told my dad I'd be married and have kids, and they'll like the baby pigs. He almost went crazy, and my mom had to go and lie down. Maybe I was wrong to tell them, but they always taught me to tell the truth."

The bell rang. Bob climbed down from his window seat and returned the pen and paper to Jonathan. He said his father was coming to see me on Open School Night next week. He was sorry for ruining the lesson.

On Open School Night, Bob's father sat by my desk and shook his head sadly. "How's my son doing?" he asked in a German accent.

"Fine," I said.

"He's killing us, breaking our hearts. Did he tell you? He wants to be a farmer."

"It's a healthy life, Mr. Stein."

"It's a disaster. We're not paying for him to go to college so he can be a pig farmer. People in our street will talk about us. It's going to kill my wife. If he wants to be a farmer, he'll have to pay for himself. We told him that. He tells us not to worry because big government programs pay for people like him to study farming. We're losing him, Mr. McCourt. Our son is dead to us. We're Jewish. We can't have a son living with pigs every day."

"I'm sorry, Mr. Stein."

♦

Six years later, I met Bob on Lower Broadway. It was a January day, but he was still wearing his Orson Welles jacket and short pants. He said, "Hi, Mr. McCourt. Great day, isn't it?"

"It's freezing, Bob."

He told me he was working for a farmer in Ohio, but he wasn't working with pigs. He decided not to because it would destroy his parents. I told him that was a good and loving decision.

He paused and looked at me. "Mr. McCourt, you never liked me, did you?"

"Never liked you? Are you joking? It was a great pleasure to have you in my class. Jonathan said you brought sunshine into the room."

Tell him the truth, McCourt. Tell him how he brightened your days, how you told your friends about him. Tell him how you admired his style, his good humor, his honesty, his bravery. If you had a son, you'd like the boy to be like him. And tell him how beautiful he was and is in every way. How you loved him then and love him now. Tell him.

I did, and he was speechless. I hugged him. "Let the people on Lower Broadway laugh at the sight of the high school teacher hugging the large Jewish Future Farmer of America," I thought. I didn't care.

♦

Ken was a Korean boy who hated his father. He had to take piano lessons although his family had no piano. His father made him practice on the kitchen table until they could afford a real piano. If he didn't practice correctly, his father hit him across the fingers with a large metal spoon. His six-year-old sister, too. When they got a real piano, his sister played a silly pop song on it. Her father was so angry that he threw her clothes on the fire.

At Stuyvesant High School, Ken obeyed his father in everything until he had to choose a college. His father wanted him to go to Harvard. Everyone in Korea knew about Harvard, the most famous university in America.

Ken said no. He wanted to go to Stanford in California. He wanted to live as far away from his father as possible. His father said no. He would not allow that. Ken said if he didn't go to Stanford, he wouldn't go to college at all. The father was going to physically attack him in the kitchen, but he was afraid of Ken. Ken was bigger and stronger. The father walked away angrily. He didn't want his son to go to Stanford. But he'd be even more ashamed if his son didn't go to college at all.

Ken wrote me from Stanford. He liked the sunshine there. College life was easier than Stuyvesant High School. There was less pressure. He'd just had a letter from his mother. She said he had to spend all his time working, and he mustn't join any clubs or do any other extra activities. If he didn't get grade A for everything, she wouldn't allow him to come home for Christmas.

Ken didn't mind. He didn't want to come home for Christmas. He came home only to see his sister.

He appeared at my classroom door a few days before Christmas and told me I'd helped him get through his last year of high school. He'd often dreamed, he told me, of killing his father. But when he went to Stanford, he began to understand his father a little more. His father knew almost no English and spent every working day and night selling fruit and vegetables. He badly wanted his children to get the education he had never had. In an English class at Stanford, Ken was asked by the professor to talk about his favorite poem. Ken remembered a poem he'd studied in my class, "My Father." While he was talking about it, he suddenly started crying in front of all the other students. The professor put his arm around Ken's shoulder and led him down the hallway to his office. He stayed an hour in the professor's office, talking and crying. The professor said it was OK. He had a father who he hadn't liked—a cruel Polish Jew. His father had almost died in a German prison camp in World War II. He'd come to California and managed a food store to pay for his three children's education. The professor said their two fathers would have a lot to talk about together, but that would never happen. The Korean grocer and Polish-Jewish food store manager could never find the words that come so easily in a university. Ken said he felt much better after talking to his professor. Now he was going to buy his father a tie for Christmas and his mother some flowers. Yeah, it was crazy buying her flowers because they sold them in the store. But there was a big difference between flowers from a Korean grocer's store and flowers from a real flower store.

He couldn't forget one thing his professor had said. The world should let the Polish-Jewish father and the Korean father sit in the sun with their wives. Ken laughed over how excited the professor became. "Just let them sit in the sun. But the world won't let them because there's nothing more dangerous than letting old men sit in the sun. They might be thinking. And it's the same with kids. Keep them busy or they might start thinking."

Chapter 20   Last Day in School

Time passes quickly. You're getting older—and aren't you a sad, weak, stupid Irishman? You teach others to write, but you know your own writing dream is dying. You tell yourself that one day one of your students will win a National Book Prize. They'll invite you to the event, and in a great acceptance speech will thank you, their teacher, for everything. You'll be asked to stand, and you'll be loudly cheered. This will be your time in the sun, your reward for thousands of lessons. Your prizewinner hugs you, and you return quietly to the streets of New York, down the stairs to your small apartment, some dry bread in the cupboard, a bottle of water in the refrigerator, a small yellow light hanging over your single bed.

A young part-time teacher sits beside me in the teachers' cafeteria. She is going to start her full-time teaching career in September, so could I offer her any advice?

"Find what you love and do it. That's my advice. It's true, I didn't always love teaching. It was too difficult. You're alone in the classroom, one man or woman in front of five classes of teenagers every day. You have to find ways of surviving. They may like you, they may even love you, but they're young. It's the business of young people to push old people off the stage. A teacher's life is similar to the life of a professional fighter. One bad fight, and that's the end of your career. But if you're smart and patient, you'll learn the tricks. It's hard but you have to make yourself comfortable in the classroom. You have to be selfish. Like on an airplane in an emergency, you must help yourself before you can help the children.

"The classroom is a difficult but exciting place. You'll never know the effect you've had on the hundreds of children you teach. You see them leaving the classroom: dreamy, impolite, smiling, admiring, puzzled. After a few years, you learn to read their minds quickly. You wouldn't exist for long in this job if you didn't. You're with the kids and, if you want to be a teacher, there's no escape. Don't expect help from the management, those people who have escaped from the classroom. They're busy going to lunch and thinking higher thoughts. It's you and the kids. So, there's the bell. See you later. Find what you love and do it."

◆

It was April and sunny outside. I wondered how many more Aprils I'd spend as a teacher. I was beginning to feel I had nothing more to say to the high school students of New York about writing or anything else. I thought I wanted to be out in the world before I was out of the world. How could I talk about writing when I'd never written a book. Didn't they wonder about that? Didn't they say, "Why does he talk so much about writing when he's never done it himself?"

It was time to stop working. I wouldn't have much money, but I could read all the books I'd missed in the last thirty years. I'd spend hours at the Forty-second Street Library, my favorite place in New York. I'd walk the streets, have a beer, talk to my friends, learn the guitar, take my daughter Maggie for dinner in Greenwich Village, write in my notebooks. Something might happen.

◆

When Guy Lind was a second-year student, he brought his umbrella to school on a snowy day. He met a friend on the second floor who also had an umbrella. They began a playful

69

fight with their umbrellas, but his friend fell and the end of his umbrella went through Guy's eye and into his brain.

They took Guy to Beth Israel Hospital across the street, and then from city to city and country to country. They even took him to Israel, where they have the most modern treatment because of all the fighting.

Guy returned to school in a wheelchair, wearing a piece of black material over one eye. After a short time, he managed to walk with the help of a walking stick. As more time passed, he didn't need the stick, and he looked completely normal except for the black cloth over his eye and an arm that he couldn't move.

It was my last day as a teacher. Guy sat listening to Rachel Blaustein talking about poems. She enjoyed reading them, but she couldn't write them. Why? Because she had nothing to write about. Everything in her life was perfect. Her parents were happy and successful. Rachel was their only child, and she was going to Harvard University. She had no problems.

Someone said, "Why can't *I* have no problems?"

Then Guy told the class about his experiences in the last two years. He'd suffered, but he wouldn't want to change anything about his past. He'd met many people in many hospitals whose lives had been completely destroyed by illness and accidents. It had made him think differently about his own problems. It had made him feel lucky. No, he wouldn't change a thing.

This was their last high school class, and mine. There were tears when Guy told his story. It reminded us all to think of the good things in our lives.

The bell rang, and they all said goodbye to me. I was told to have a good life. I wished them the same. As I left the classroom for the last time, a voice called out to me.

"Hey, Mr. McCourt, you should write a book."

I'll try.

ACTIVITIES

Chapters 1–3

Before you read

1 Read the Introduction to the book and then answer these questions.

   a For how many years was Frank McCourt a teacher?

   b Where did McCourt first read Shakespeare?

   c How many books has McCourt written?

   d How old was he when his first book appeared?

2 Look at the Word List at the back of the book.

   a Which are words for jobs in schools and colleges?

   b Which words describe types and levels of education?

   c Which are words for things that you can buy in a store?

3 Discuss these questions with another student.

   a What is the education system like in your country? What types of school and college are there? How do students succeed or fail? How are teachers trained?

   b Which of these qualities are most important for a successful school teacher? Which are least important? Why?

   intelligence   a sense of humor   toughness   creativity

   a good speaking voice   patience   a smart appearance

   What other qualities would you add to a description of a successful teacher?

While you read

4 Are these sentences about Mr. McCourt true (T) or false (F)?

   a He wrote his first book while he was a teacher.   .....

   b He thinks that teachers deserve more respect.   .....

   c His students at McKee High School don't listen
      to him at first.   .....

   d A student throws a sandwich at him.   .....

   e He tells the principal why he ate the sandwich.   .....

   f His students are bored by his stories.   .....

   g His students think that his answer about sheep is funny.   .....

   h Parents complain about his sheep joke.   .....

| **i** | He hopes to be a school principal one day. | ..... |
| **j** | He tells his students to sleep on the floor. | ..... |

5 Discuss these questions.

  a Which of these words describe Mr. McCourt? Give reasons for your answers.

    confident proud surprised guilty imaginative angry nervous bored

  b How different is McKee Vocational High School from your school? Which school do you like more? Why?

6 Work with another student. Have this conversation between the principal and an angry parent.

  Student A: You are an angry parent. You do not think that Mr. McCourt is a good teacher. Tell the principal why.

  Student B: You are the principal. Tell the parent why you think that Mr. McCourt is a good teacher. Make excuses for his behavior.

Chapters 4–6

Before you read

7 How will these be important in the next three chapters? What do you think?

  a Frank McCourt's childhood **b** the students' parents

While you read

8 Number these events from Mr. McCourt's life in the correct order, from 1 to 8.

a	He has a girlfriend called June.	.....
b	He is shouted at by an angry parent.	.....
c	He joins the army.	.....
d	He goes to university.	.....
e	A parent criticizes his teaching.	.....
f	He leaves Ireland.	.....
g	His students learn a new word.	.....
h	He works on the docks.	.....

After you read

9 Discuss whether Mr. McCourt likes these people. Give reasons for your answers.

    a his parents

    b The Professor of Education at New York University

    c June

    d Norma

    e Paulie's mother

    f Ron

    g Kenny Ball

10 Who says these words? Who are they talking to? What are they talking about?

    a "That was wrong of your mother."

    b "Forget the docks."

    c "That's not the Harry we know."

    d "This place is a madhouse."

    e "Forget the storytelling."

    f "Why did John go to the store?"

11 Discuss these questions with another student. What do you think?

    a Is storytelling in class a waste of time? Why (not)?

    b Is Mr. McCourt right not to be honest with parents on Open Day? Why (not)?

    c Why does Mr. McCourt feel proud at the end of Chapter 6? Is he right to feel proud? Why (not)?

Chapters 7–9

Before you read

12 Discuss these questions.

    a Will Mr. McCourt want to stay at McKee Vocational High School, do you think? Why (not)?

    b What do you think an "excuse note" tells a teacher?

    c What can a school—and a teacher—do with a child who is a real troublemaker?

13 Match the people on the left with the sentence endings on
   the right.

a	Mikey Dolan	**1)**	likes long words.
b	Lisa Quinn	**2)**	marries Mr. McCourt.
c	Martin Wolfson	**3)**	defends Eve's behavior.
d	Kevin Dunne	**4)**	is Mr. McCourt's friend.
e	Barbara Sadlar	**5)**	congratulates Mr. McCourt.
f	Alberta Small	**6)**	is very smart.
g	Herbert Miller	**7)**	becomes classroom manager.
h	Freddie Bell	**8)**	forges excuse notes.

After you read

14 What is Mr. McCourt's purpose in using these in his classes?
   How successful is he?

   a Adam and Eve

   b jars of paint

   c advice about simple language

   d the college library

   e gun control

15 In these chapters, what is Mr. McCourt's

   a greatest success?

   b biggest mistake?

   c saddest experience?

   d worst failure?

16 Discuss these questions with another student. What do you think?

   a Compare your answers to question 15. Do you agree?
      Why (not)?

   b Would you behave differently in these situations if *you* were the
      teacher? Why (not)?

Chapters 10–11

Before you read

17 In the next chapter, Mr. McCourt leaves the college and goes to
   another high school. Why do you think he does this? Will he be
   happier there? Why (not)?

18 Circle the correct word(s) in these sentences about Mr. McCourt.

    a He *has / wants* to leave the college.

    b His wife thinks he is *dishonest / lazy*.

    c He says that a ballpoint pen is like a *sentence / verb*.

    d He leaves Fashion High School because he has trouble with *a student / the principal*.

    e His students at Seward Park High School are more interested in *reading / speaking*.

    f He thinks that Nancy Chu is *crazy / interesting*.

After you read

19 Answer these questions.

    a Why doesn't Mr. McCourt's head of department at Fashion High School like him?

    b Why does Mr. McCourt hit Hector?

    c What does Mr. McCourt's head of department think is a good idea?

    d What problems does Hector have?

    e Who helps Mr. McCourt to find the job at Seward Park?

    f Who likes American musicals?

    g How does Mr. McCourt feel about his students at Seward Park High School?

    h How do the students feel after Nancy Chu talks about her mother?

20 Work with another student. Have this imaginary conversation between Mr. McCourt and his wife.

    Student A: You are Alberta. You want your husband to take more examinations and stay at the college. Tell him why.

    Student B: You are Mr. McCourt. You don't want to take any more examinations. Tell your wife why.

Chapters 12–14

Before you read

21 In the next chapters, Mr. McCourt takes his students on trips to see a movie and a play. What problems do you think he will have? Which trip do you think the students will enjoy more? Why?

22 Underline the words that are wrong. Write the correct words.

    a Serena's sister stole money from a store. ....

    b Mr. McCourt takes twenty girls to a movie theater. ....

    c On the subway, Mr. McCourt wants to criticize
his students. ....

    d When the movie ends, the girls leave. ....

    e He also takes the girls to see *Macbeth*. ....

    f After she goes to Georgia, Serena writes
Mr. McCourt a letter. ....

    g Serena wants to teach high school students. ....

    h Andrew is a popular, pale, thin, red-haired boy. ....

    i Andrew's mother used to be Mr. McCourt's teacher. ....

After you read

23 Which of these words describe Mr. McCourt in these chapters?
Why?

angry   excited   grateful   happy   surprised   shocked

24 Discuss these statements with another student. Do you agree with
them? Why (not)?

    a "School trips to the movies are a waste of time."

    b "Mr. McCourt is a good, experienced teacher."

    c "Mr. McCourt is happier now than he used to be."

Chapters 15–17

Before you read

25 In the next chapter, Mr. McCourt decides to go to Ireland to study
for a doctorate. Is this a good idea? Why (not)?

While you read

26 Does Mr. McCourt do these things? Write *yes* or *no*.

    a He gets his doctorate. .....

    b He goes back to Fashion High School. .....

    c He teaches at a good quality school. .....

    d He wants to stop teaching. .....

    e He helps a girl with a personal problem. .....

    f He stays with an artist. .....

g He answers all his students' questions. .....

h He apologizes to a student. .....

After you read

27 Why is Mr. McCourt unhappy about:

    a his time in Ireland?

    b the new principal at Seward Park High School?

    c substitute teaching?

    d his weekends?

    e his marriage?

    f the success of his creative writing classes?

    g the "dinner conversation" with Daniel?

28 Which of these statements would Mr. McCourt agree with, do you think? Why? Do you agree with them? Why (not)? Discuss your answers with another student.

    a "It is more important to be rich and famous than to be a poor schoolteacher."

    b "Teachers should help students with personal problems."

    c "Respect is more important than happiness."

Chapters 18–20

Before you read

29 Discuss these questions.

    a How do you think Open School Day at Stuyvesant High School will be different from Open School Day at McKee Vocational High School (Chapter 5)?

    b Will Mr. McCourt be happy or sad when he finally stops teaching? Why?

While you read

30 Who are these sentences about?

    a He wants to study the guitar. ....

    b They only care about money. ....

    c His father is very religious. ....

    d His father is afraid of him. ....

    e His father almost died in World War II. ....

    f He compares teachers to fighters. ....

g He loses his eye in an accident. ....

h She can't write poems. ....

After you read

31 Discuss these questions with another student.

    a What problems do these people have?

      Stanley Bob Stein Ken Guy Lind Rachel Blaustein

    b Whose problems are the most serious? Why?

    c Whose problems are the least serious? Why?

    d What advice would you give to

      Stanley's parents? Bob's father? Ken's father?

Writing

32 Write a school inspector's report on McKee Vocational High School (Chapters 2–9). Write about the teachers and students, the guidance counseling, the principal, and the classes, and make suggestions for improvement.

33 Imagine that Barbara Sadlar's parents (Chapter 9) have written an angry letter to Mr. McCourt, saying that they can't afford to send Barbara to college. They want her to be a hairdresser and to start earning money. Write a reply from Mr. McCourt.

34 Imagine that you are Serena (Chapter 13). Write your first letter to Mr. McCourt from Georgia.

35 Write a letter from Frank McCourt in Ireland (Chapter 15) to his wife. Why does he want to return home?

36 Write a letter from Alberta Small to her best friend. She wants to leave her husband (Chapter 16). Explain why.

37 Write four or five sentences about each these students. Do they like Mr. McCourt. Why (not)?

  Mikey Dolan (Chapter 7)   Freddie Bell (Chapter 9),

  Hector (Chapter 10)   Andrew (Chapter 14)

  Bob Stein (Chapter 19)

38 If you were a teacher, where would you choose to teach—at McKee Vocational High School or at Stuyvesant High School? Why?

39 Imagine that you are Frank McCourt. Write about your saddest and your happiest memories of teaching. Say why you have chosen them.

40 Do you agree with this statement? Why (not)?
"Open Days for parents are a waste of everybody's time."

41 Write about *your* favorite teacher at school or college. Why will you always remember him/her?

WORD LIST

ballpoint pen (n) a pen with a very small ball at the end that makes the ink run smoothly onto paper

beg (v) to ask for something (for example, food, money, or help) in an urgent way

career (n) a type of job or a profession that you have trained for and plan to do for a long time

cheer (v) to shout happily because you like something that has just happened

creative (adj) good at thinking of new ideas or ways of doing things

degree (n) something that a student receives when they successfully finish a university course

dock (n) a place where heavy things are taken on and off ships

doctorate (n) the highest level of university degree

forge (v) to copy something illegally so that people think it is real

gibberish (n) meaningless language

guidance counselor (n) a person in a school or college who advises students with personal problems

handkerchief (n) a small piece of cloth used for drying your nose or eyes

hot dog (n) a long piece of cooked meat in a long piece of bread

hug (v) to put your arms around someone in a friendly way and hold them tightly

ignore (v) to pay no attention to something or someone

lecturer (n) a teacher at college or university

miserable (adj) very unhappy

monitor (n) a person who watches a situation carefully to make sure that nothing goes wrong

principal (n) the most important person in a school or college

psychology (n) the scientific study of the mind and how it works

research (n/v) serious, detailed study of a subject to find new information

respect (n/v) admiration for someone because of their knowledge, skill, or success

shoelace (n) a thin piece of string or leather that you use to tie your shoes